FAMOUS REGIMENTS

The Loyal Regiment

FAMOUS REGIMENTS

Edited by
Lt-General Sir Brian Horrocks

The Loyal Regiment
(North Lancashire)
(The 47th and 81st Regiments of Foot)

by
Michael Langley

Leo Cooper Ltd, London

First published in Great Britain in 1976 by
Leo Cooper Ltd,
196 Shaftesbury Avenue,
London WC2H 8JL

Copyright © 1976 by Michael Langley

Foreword Copyright © 1976 by
Field-Marshal Sir Gerald Templer

ISBN 0 85052 075 4

Printed in Great Britain
by Clarke, Doble & Brendon Ltd,
Plymouth

To the memory of
all ranks of
The 47th and 81st Foot,
The Loyal North Lancashire Regiment
and The Loyal Regiment
who died in the service
of the Crown

Contents

	Preface	xv
1	1741: 'By Beat of Drum...'	1
2	Wolfe's Own	5
3	The War of American Independence	13
4	The Loyal Lincoln Volunteers	20
5	Napoleon is Taught a Lesson	23
6	With Moore at Corunna	28
7	The Ubiquitous Regiments	35
8	The Crimean War	41
9	India	48
10	The Defence of Kimberley	51
11	The First World War	59
12	Years of Relative Peace, 1919–1939	79
13	The Second World War: Defence of the Dunkirk Perimeter	83
14	The Second World War: Defeat into Victory	88
15	Into the Atomic Age	104
	Epilogue	110
	Appendix A: Important Dates in the History of The Loyal Regiment	113
	Appendix B: The Regimental March	116
	Appendix C: Battle Honours of The Loyal Regiment	118

Illustrations

1 Gen Sir John Mordaunt   *facing page* 44
2 Col John Hale   44
3 The Battle of Quebec   44
4 Gen Albemarle Bertie   45
5 Major-Gen Sir James Kempt   45
6 The Battle of Maida   45
7 The Maida Tortoise   76
8 The 47th in Burma in 1826   76
9 Major R. T. Farren   77
10 Pte J. McDermond at the Battle of Inkerman   77

between pages 92 and 93

11 The Battle of Ali Masjid
12 Loyals in captured pickelhaube (*The Imperial War Museum*)
13 Major-Gen R. G. Kekewich
14 Lt W. A. Sandys-Clarke, VC
15 The 1st Battalion, The Loyal Regiment, on the North-West Frontier
16 Guard duties in London (*Provincial Newspapers Ltd*)
17 The presentation of new colours to The Queen's Lancashire Regiment
18 HM The Queen with Brig G. A. Rimbault (*Soldier*)

Foreword

by Field-Marshal Sir Gerald Templer
KG, GCB, GCMG, KBE, DSO, DCL, LLD

It was just over twenty years ago that I wrote the Foreword
to the third volume of the Regimental history, covering the two
World Wars and the years between and just after. In it, I hope
I made my feelings clear as to the qualities of the Lancashire-
man as a soldier, and also of my admiration for the Regiment
whose cap badge I had the honour to wear for nearly ten
years.

It is not therefore an easy task to write something new in this
Foreword to Michael Langley's short history, excellent as it is,
though necessarily compressed. This has one advantage in that
it throws up certain facts in strong relief.

It is of course invidious to attempt to compare the fighting or
peacetime records of individual Regiments. All have their ups
and downs over the centuries, and all have episodes in their history of which they are immensely proud – and rightly so. It
seems to me however that the Loyals have had more than their
share of service overseas in areas where trouble was cooking
or had just broken out, and in the geographical spread of their
overseas stations in every part of the globe. I think that few
Regiments could better their luck in that respect.

And then of course they also seem to have had the habit of
finding themselves as the only British troops to be stationed in
some area where bullets were likely to be flying. This habit is
often uncomfortable at the time, even if exciting and interesting.
It is a happy state, for after all it is the job of the Land Forces
of the Crown – and the other fighting services – to do the
Sovereign's business when necessary.

My admiration and affection for the Loyals is as strong or
stronger than ever it was, especially since I saw at first hand the

xii

way in which they accepted their amalgamation and the splendid Regiment which was born in its place.

How much I agree with the sentence written by the last Colonel of the Regiment in his epilogue: 'It was an honour to have been a Loyal.' Indeed it was.

FAMOUS REGIMENTS

The Loyal Regiment

Preface

I was once taught the precept, 'never complain and never explain', but in the present case I feel that some explanation is owed to the veterans of The Loyal Regiment because this book should have been finished long ago. For this delay I apologize to all members of the Regiment, but whilst much of the book was soon written, the completion of the later chapters was protracted by illness which has held up my progress for the last year.

I am most grateful for advice to Field-Marshal Sir Gerald Templer, KG, GCB, GCMG, KBE, DSO, who served with the Loyals for nearly a decade between the wars, and was decorated with the DSO whilst with them in Palestine.

The Regiment's last Colonel, Brig G. A. Rimbault, CBE, DSO, MC, has shown rare patience, quite apart from having given me advice on many matters which he was singularly able to provide. I owe him my sincere thanks, and to both Brigadier and Mrs Rimbault for their hospitality. I am also indebted to several of the Brigadier's former comrades, notably Brig M. H. H. Collins, MBE and Brig Mordaunt Elrington, DSO, OBE (whose ancestry, as I have stated, can be traced directly to Gen Mordaunt, the founder of the 47th, and Lt-Col Elrington of the early nineteenth century) who gave me invaluable first-hand advice from his experience as the former Commanding Officer of the 2nd Loyals in Malaya and Singapore in 1941–42. Brig (then Capt) J. W. A. Stares, CBE, DSO, was Adjutant of the 1st Loyals just prior to, and during, the evacuation from Dunkirk. His advice on that campaign, therefore, has been of enormous help. From the Regiment's historians I have, of course, derived great assistance; notably from the surviving historian, Capt C. G. T. Dean, MBE, who wrote the Regiment's history from 1919 to 1953. Substantial help has naturally also come from the home of the Regiment, and I am much indebted to Lt-Col J. Jeffries, MBE, and Lt-Col P. Rogers, JP, and their colleagues at the Regimental Museum, Fulwood Barracks, Preston.

For advice throughout I am, as always, grateful to my friend and
agent, John Johnson.

Michael Langley
Reigate, December 1975.

CHAPTER 1

1741: 'By Beat of Drum ...'

'GEORGE R

'These are to authorize you by beat of drum or otherwise to raise volunteers in any County or part of our Kingdom of Great Britain for a Regiment of Foot under your command, which is to consist of ten companies of three sergeants, three corporals, two drummers and seventy effective private men in each company, besides commissioned officers: and all Magistrates, Justices of the Peace, Constables and others of our Civil officers whom it may concern are hereby required to be assisting unto you in providing quarters, impressing carriages and otherwise as there shall be occasion.

'Given at Our Court of St James's this third day of January, 1741, in the fourteenth year of Our Reign.

'By His Majesty's Commands.

(sd) WILL. YOUNG'

'To our Trusty and Well-beloved John Mordaunt Esq, Colonel of one of our Regiments of Foot, or to the Officer or Officers appointed by you to raise Volunteers for Our said Regiments.'

So, by concise command, was created the embryo of The Loyal Regiment. There was nothing unusual about its formation. The British Army, gradually becoming formalized from the *ad hoc* basis on which its earliest regiments had been raised to strengthen the throne after the Civil War, was still very much privately owned and trained. Col John Mordaunt, like others so charged, was a wealthy landowner of military experience who could freely afford to give of his time and wealth to the service of the Crown. And these were the days when Crown and country needed protection: William and Mary, heavily committed in Ireland; Anne, threatened by France and Spain over the issue of the Spanish succession; George I, threatened by the tenuous succession of the Hanoverians; George II, threatened by France in the War of the Austrian Succession and the Seven Years' War; and all these monarchs threatened by the menace of the Stuart pretenders, themselves encouraged by Britain's enemies on the continent. John Mordaunt had, indeed, to be 'trusty and well-beloved'.

But the Regiment can also claim a remote connection with one of six regiments of Marines, raised in 1739 – the year when Britain had declared war against Spain over the latter's alleged right to search British ships in the West Indies, and the Spaniards' provocative act in removing Captain Jenkins's ear. Marine regiments had particular advantages over the Army; the pay was better, the service wider and the recruitment easier, but, above all, the marines lacked the stigma which still attached itself to the soldiery from the days of Cromwell's brutal military expedients. In 1739, when the Army numbered only 18,000 men, every means was used to swell the ranks, and every individual soldier counted. Of these six regiments, the 4th (Col Wynyard's Marines) was that which eventually took precedence in the Line as the 47th and had served in the ill-fated attack on Carthagina in 1741. And here is the tenuous link with the Loyals, for on the disbandment of Wynyard's Marines at the Peace of Aix-la-Chapelle in 1748, Mordaunt's Regiment, which had been ranked as the 58th, now took precedence as the 47th. But by this time the Infantry Regiment had already distinguished itself in the Second Jacobite Rising, the 'Forty-Five'.

But what more do we know about Mordaunt and his comrades? Mordaunt himself had joined the Army on 25 August, 1721, as an ensign in the 3rd Foot Guards (later The Scots Guards), had become successively captain and lieutenant-colonel, and was promoted to colonel to raise the 47th on 15 January, 1741. But he was with his Regiment for a remarkably short time, being transferred to the colonelcy of the 18th Foot (later The Royal Irish Regiment, disbanded in 1922) in March, 1742. Eventually, he rose, through other regiments, to the rank of General in 1770, ten years before his death. He commanded brigades at the Battles of Falkirk, Culloden and Val, and the land forces at the controversial Rochefort expedition in 1757.

Apart from Mordaunt, the 47th consisted of the establishment usual in those days of a lieutenant-colonel, a major, seven captains, ten lieutenants, nine ensigns, a chaplain and two surgeons. It was also quite common – in fact, almost the custom – for a regiment to be raised in a different part of Britain from that with which it eventually became associated; and the dire need for swift recruitment often involved a degree of itinerant press ganging with fifes and drums amongst the occupants of ale houses, and forcible enlistment from the prisons. The 47th was raised in Scotland where strong forces were needed against possible Jacobite insurrection. The Royal Army's inroads into Scottish recruitment did a great deal to undermine the clan system and subvert its threat when insurrection returned for the second time in 1745. But a warrant dated 21 February, 1741, ordered 'a draft of fifty men and two drummers to be sent from Colonel Pulteney's Regiment to Colonel Mordaunt's at Birmingham'. But we learn that the 47th was soon back in Scotland; another warrant of 7 April, 1742, having ordered a draft of ten men and three drummers to be sent to Col Lowther's Marines at Edinburgh.

Mordaunt was succeeded by Col Peregrine Lascelles, whose twelve-year tenure of the colonelcy enabled the Regiment to progress at a steady pace under an avuncular eye. Having served already in the 1st Foot Guards (later the Grenadiers) Lascelles maintained the command of the 47th whilst rising to the rank of lieutenant-general in January, 1758, and through many notable campaigns.

The 47th was thus particularly fortunate, not only in the unbroken length of this command but also in the character of its second Colonel who is described on a tablet at St Mary's Church, Whitby, as 'Bountiful to his soldiers, a Father to his officers, a man of truth and principle, in short, an Honest Man'. Such was the commander who took his Regiment into action for the first time, behind the fifes and drums northward through

4

the Lowlands to meet the minions of Prince Charles Edward Stuart in 1745.[1]

[1]Although Lascelles held the command of the 47th from 1742 until 1762, the dates of his colonelcy begin a year after Mordaunt's removal to the 18th Foot and continue for ten years after his retirement from active command. He was thus Colonel of the Regiment from 17 March, 1743, until 2 April, 1772, when he was succeeded by Lt-Gen Lord Guy Dorchester. Lascelles' tenure of this office must therefore have been unsurpassed by any other regimental Colonel, at least during the eighteenth century.

CHAPTER 2

Wolfe's Own

THE 47th, then, was in action as one of the regiments sent to contain the rebellion of the Young Pretender in 1745, and although it showed great manoeuvrability over rough country the King's Army was beaten at Prestonpans by the clever rebel. But Colonel Lascelles and his men were absolved from any blame.

Wearers of the tie of The Loyal Regiment will know that the black stripe, incorporated in the design, has a special significance in their regimental history. The Loyals shared with several other regiments the interweaving of black in the lace, but they alone bear the nickname, 'Wolfe's Own', for close support at Quebec of their gallant commander whose death is still mourned by the descendants of those regiments which stormed the Heights of Abraham. By the time Wolfe's campaign had ended with this famous action, the 47th had already served in Nova Scotia and Canada for nine years and had won its first battle honour at Louisburg.

In 1746 the Regiment moved back from Scotland to England and in the early autumn it furnished a draft to complete the 30th Regiment (later the 1st East Lancashire Regiment) which sailed in an expedition against L'Orient. New men were recruited to make up the regimental strength. Again, in 1747, the Regiment seems to have supplemented the strength of another regiment, bound for service under the East India Company, whilst the Regiment as a whole was quartered in Dublin.

The Peace of Aix-la-Chapelle nearly saw the disbandment of the Loyals' forbear altogether. But at the demise of the old 42nd and all those marine regiments raised in 1739–40 the 58th, as has been mentioned, became the 47th. The narrowness of its survival will be appreciated when it is realized that of the Line regiments only 1–49 (after numerical reorganization) were kept on the Establishment. Thirty thousand men remained on the British List, two-thirds of whom were to serve in Britain and one-third in the colonies, whilst the rest (thirty-seven rather under-strength battalions) were transferred to the Irish Establishment. Of these, according to the *Gentlemen's Magazine* for October, 1748, we find one identified simply as 'Lascell'.

But the new 47th seems to have survived the terrible fate of stagnation on the edge of the peat bogs of Ireland, for in the following year it sailed via that military backwater for service in Nova Scotia where it was quartered in Halifax. And from here it was well placed to take a leading role in the capture of Canada from the French and the culmination of this campaign in perhaps the most famous battle between Blenheim and Waterloo.

Nova Scotia was in the anomalous position of having been settled by Frenchmen, and yet ceded by France to Britain at the Treaty of Utrecht in 1713. Thus 'Acadia', as the French called it, was inevitably a thorn in Britain's colonial flesh, and the French in Canada ensured that this state of affairs was perpetuated by fermenting boundary disputes and guerrilla warfare across the frontier. In 1748, at the Treaty of Aix-la-Chapelle, Louisburg (the capital of Breton Island, adjoining to the north-east) was returned to France, but in the following year 2,500 emigrants were sent out from Britain to settle in the south of the Nova Scotian peninsula as a counterpoise to the new French naval base at Louisburg. The French inhabitants, resenting this intrusion, rose at Halifax, the old capital at Annapolis Royal and elsewhere.

At this moment the 47th reached Halifax. In August, 1750, the new Lieutenant-Governor of the Province of Annapolis, Col Charles Lawrence, was ordered to check the new threat at Chignecto and he duly took with him the entire 47th, and 300 men of the 45th (later the 1st Sherwood Foresters). 'I never saw a detachment of better men', wrote Lord Cornwallis, the Governor of Acadia, as he watched them depart on their mission; whilst of the accomplishment of that mission we read in Murdoch's *History of Nova Scotia* that 'notwithstanding (the

French) opposition the gallant and intrepid behaviour of the English beat them out, although the defenders are said to have outnumbered them sixfold . . .' The English regiments used the cool and deliberate tactics which made the British Army so renowned at Dettingen and on many other European battle-fields – they advanced in impeccable order almost to the enemy's entrenchments before delivering the most accurate and withering fire, and forcing the French to break and run. Thereafter the Regiment formed the garrison at Fort Lawrence.

From early in 1750 the lieutenant-colonelcy of the 47th passed to the Hon Robert Monckton, Wolfe's most trusted subordinate, who took command of the Regiment in Nova Scotia. The following year, incidentally, was that in which regiments ceased to be identified by the names of their Colonels, but by their numerical precedence only, although, of course, the old practice died hard. By May, 1755, a year before the outbreak of the Seven Years' War, it had been decided to co-ordinate resistance to the scattered but fierce French nationalists at Chignecto, Beausejour, Fort Gaspereau and elsewhere. Monckton, reinforced by troops from New York, was placed in command of the British army which was harassed as much by the terrain and the Indians, known to be working under French orders, as by the French themselves. By the end of the year those objectives had been taken, and Monckton said of his Regiment, 'The Regulars under the command of Captains Hussey, Hale and Spital, as also the other officers and men, ever showed themselves diligent and behaved much to their credit.' Since the conquered French refused to take any but a qualified oath of allegiance it was decided to have them distributed among other British colonies, an unpleasant task which fell to the 47th and other regiments of the Acadian garrison. Not until the Peace of Paris in 1763 was France obliged to hand Nova Scotia over to Britain. But now, in May, 1756, with the Seven Years' War formally declared, a force was being prepared for the final capture of Louisburg and Breton Island.

Lord Loudoun, whose Highland Regiment had fought with the 47th during the 'Forty-Five', was sent from Britain with specific orders to capture Louisburg and Quebec, but his dilatoriness caused Pitt to replace him by Gen Jeffrey Amherst. The fleet was commanded by Admiral Boscawen, and by May, 1758 the entire force arrived at Halifax. The army consisted of twelve regiments, including the 47th and two battalions of the 60th Rifles. Facing them at Louisburg were about three thousand seasoned French troops in twenty-four companies of marines, two companies of artillery and four of infantry, and seven hundred Canadians.

Not since the capture of Gibraltar and the subsequent operations in the Mediterranean had such an elaborate amphibious invasion been conducted. It took the form of a pincer movement, with three divisions landing at various points astride the objective. The left division under Wolfe, which was to pack the punch, landed at Freshwater Cove and included the Grenadier Companies of the 47th, whilst the rest of the Regiment helped to comprise the right division under Lawrence, now promoted to Brigadier-General. The entire regimental strength of the 47th was nearer that of the modern battalion, for we learn that it consisted of a lieutenant-colonel, a major, five captains, fifteen lieutenants, nine ensigns, an adjutant, a quartermaster, a surgeon, two surgeon's mates, thirty-eight sergeants, eighteen drummers and 856 rank and file. From now on the Regiment was to consist of this greatly increased strength.

Impeded by the tide as well as by stern French resistance, Wolfe, particularly, had a difficult landing on 8 June. He was followed by the divisions of Lawrence and Whitmore. It was ten days before the siege guns could be landed, but with great dash Wolfe's Grenadier Companies, commanded by Lt-Col Hale of the 47th, now stormed, captured and held the French shore batteries, whilst the other divisions established themselves and the invaders drew closer to the fortress. Eventually, on 26 June, the last French battery on the ramparts was silenced and the French commander capitulated. Five thousand six hundred and thirty-seven French and Canadian prisoners were taken – this figure must have included many armed civilians – whilst the booty included 221 cannon, eighteen mortars, 15,000 stand of arms, eleven stand of Colours and much else. The French lost over a thousand men, whilst the British casualties were only twenty-one officers and 150 men killed, and thirty officers and 320 men wounded – mostly during the initial stages. Of these, despite the fact that they were in the thick of the fighting, the 47th lost only nine killed and thirty wounded. Whitmore remained as Governor of Louisburg, Amherst proceeded to Boston on 14 September with five regiments, including the 47th, and Wolfe sailed for England but returned the following spring to command the operation against Quebec.

The capture of Quebec was only one branch of a three-pronged campaign to wrest Canada from the French, and it is often forgotten how nearly, at one stage, Wolfe came to irretrievably miscalculating his attack. A major-general at the age of thirty-three and killed at the moment of victory; these factors won him an immortal name. In actual fact he was, at that time, already mortally ill with tuberculosis.

Quebec was, until the era of modern warfare, the supreme achievement of a bold and successful amphibious assault, led by a former marine officer (later of the 20th Foot) who had been Quartermaster to Mordaunt during the unfortunate Rochefort expedition. With the help of that outstanding coastal navigator, Vice-Admiral Sir Charles Saunders, Wolfe considered various points at which to land his force. For two-and-a-half months, from early June, 1759, Saunders and Wolfe sailed beneath the high cliffs of the north-western shore of the St Lawrence, trying to entice Montcalm from his secure positions above. Eventually, on 3 September, Wolfe abandoned his third camp at the mouth of the Montmorency River and sailed south-westward beyond the St Charles River and the citadel of Quebec itself. Suddenly, on 12 September, he secretly decided upon his route of approach behind the French and up a narrow, barely defended, path to the Heights of Abraham. Having discovered the way up, he was rowed back down the St Lawrence, it is reliably recorded, reciting the whole of Gray's *Elegy* and then announcing to his surprised colleagues: 'Gentlemen, I would rather have written those lines than take Quebec'.

But the fate of Canada was sealed next day. At 2 am on 13 September the stealthy British landed below the Heights. The 47th had been in close attendance on Wolfe throughout the protracted operation, particularly in the landings on the Montmorency. Among the Regiment's earlier casualties is recorded the name of Sgt Ned Botwood, a ballad writer, whose song, *Hot Stuff*, was perhaps the best loved ballad of the day in the British Army. Even today it is still played to evoke the spirit of Wolfe's army. Once the Plains of Abraham had been reached, detachments of the 47th were detailed by Wolfe to hunt down the Red Indian marksmen and other dissidents who imperilled the British.

The 47th held a position to the right of the main Montreal–Quebec road, sharing the centre of the Line with a Highland regiment (of no direct heir today), the 43rd (later the 1st Oxfordshire and Buckinghamshire Light Infantry) and Wolfe's Headquarters. Time now favoured the British who thoroughly prepared themselves; but it was 9 am before Montcalm began to form his line. An hour later the French advanced, but were only forty yards from the positions of the eight British regiments when they were met by accurate and impregnable firepower. Lt-Col Knox, commanding the 43rd, recorded that 'when the General formed the line of battle he ordered the regiments to load with an extra ball. The 43rd and 47th in the centre, being little affected by the oblique fire of the enemy, gave them with great calmness as remarkable a close and heavy discharge as I ever saw performed at a private field of exercise'. Even the French described it as a *'coup de canon'*.

The clearing of the smoke from the scene revealed a completely shattered French line, trying here and there to muster resistance. Then, as one man, the British rose with the bayonet. Brig-Gen Townshend, who was later to be Wolfe's successor, wrote in his despatch: 'It was at this moment that each corps seemed in a manner to exert itself with a view to its own peculiar character. The Grenadiers (*Author's note:* That is, the brigaded Grenadier Companies of those regiments concerned), Bragg's (later the 1st Glosters), Lascelles' pressed on with their bayonets.' And a staff officer afterwards wrote that 'our regiments that sustained the brunt of the action were Bragg's, Lascelles' and the Highlanders, the two former had not a bayonet or the latter a broadsword untinged with blood.'

Wolfe had already been hit twice when he went forward to some high ground on the right where he had placed an advance post of the Louisburg Grenadiers. Here he was hit a third time in the chest, walked about a hundred yards to the rear and lay down. When told by a staff officer that the French had given way everywhere he smiled and murmured with his last breath, 'Now I die contented'.

Then Brig-Gen Monckton was shot through the lungs beside his old regiment, his beloved 47th. But they and the 58th (later the 2nd Northamptonshires) did not halt in their pursuit of the French until they were close to the St Louis and St Jean Gates of the City. Townshend, who had assumed command of the 47th, laid siege to Quebec and, with his Regiment, burst in upon the French. As if this were not enough, he then reconnoitred with the Navy and had the City virtually encircled. To him, more than any other, the final capitulation was due. Later that day, as he was being pursued back to the St Louis Gate by the 47th, Montcalm was mortally wounded.

Meanwhile Hale, who had replaced Monckton as Lieutenant-Colonel of the 47th, was entrusted with the despatches to London. Hale, a wealthy and ambitious man and a versatile soldier, left the 47th soon after his return in order to raise the famous 17th Lancers (now the 17th/21st Lancers; then as the 18th Light Dragoons), and the famous skull and crossbones, with the motto 'Death or Glory', was coined by Hale to commemorate the brave action of Wolfe at Quebec.

As for Hale's old regiment, the 47th, the War Office at Horse Guards expressed its appreciation of their noble service at Quebec by signifying Queen Victoria's grant of 'Quebec' to the Colours of The Loyal North Lancashire Regiment on 29 April, 1882 – one hundred and twenty-three years later! But such delays were not uncommon, and the battle had become a great tradition in the Regiment long before its name was paraded by the 47th on national and regimental occasions; and for many years it had been known by the sobriquet, 'Wolfe's Own', for no other regiment had done more to achieve that victory.

The capture of Quebec, of course, was the most outstanding victory, though not the culmination of the Seven Years' War in North America. In April, 1760, the French under Gen François de Lévis led an expedition from Montreal to try to recapture Quebec, but the siege was broken by the arrival of a British naval squadron. Now the British columns converged on Montreal, moving down the St Lawrence from Oswego under Amherst, under Col William Haviland, moving from Crown Point down the Richelieu River, and under Brig-Gen James Murray, with the Quebec command, up the St Lawrence. Among this force was the 47th which continued to uphold the pre-eminent reputation it had won under Wolfe whose most senior and trusted subordinates – Monckton, Townshend and Hale – had all belonged to the Regiment.

On 8 September, 1760, the French under Governor Vaudreuil capitulated to Amherst, and the Dominion of Canada passed to Britain.

CHAPTER 3

The War of American Independence

THE Regiment was soon back in America, but this time
without the combined brilliance of Chatham and Wolfe.
Now it was Britain's destiny to be hampered by inept
government, rendering even more impotent the luckless but in-
different leadership of her army in the American Colonies.

After service mainly in Ireland the 47th, according to the
Army List for 1773, was ordered to America as one of the
fourteen regiments (of only 10,000 men altogether) garrisoned
along the entire eastern seaboard from Quebec to Pensacola in
Florida. Britain had indulged in her usual dangerous practice of
severe troop reduction in peacetime. When the 47th reached
New Jersey, only 457 strong, the Stamp Act had already been
reimposed six years earlier, and revolution was becoming daily
more imminent.

Gen Gage had replaced Amherst, and by 1775 he had concentrated eleven infantry regiments, including the 47th, in and
around the threatening town of Boston. In May seven more
battalions reinforced the garrison, and on the 25th they were
joined by Major-Generals Howe, Clinton and Burgoyne. At last,
on 19 April, the collision came, and the Grenadier and Light
Companies of the 47th were there to witness it.

Gage had information that the colonists had built a munitions
dump at Concord near Lexington, and he detailed a force under
one Col Smith to destroy it. Passing *en route* some colonial
militia who were drilling on the village green at Lexington on
the Boston–Concord road, the patrol suddenly came under
sporadic fire and casualties occurred on both sides. The dump
was duly destroyed, but now the countryside was alive with
militiamen and snipers and Col Smith and his force struggled
for fourteen hours to cover the remaining six miles back to
Lexington, where they were joined by a relief column under

B

Major-Gen Lord Percy which contained the rest of the 47th, some marines, two guns and two other regiments. Through invisible bands of snipers, who pursued them to the outskirts of Boston until repelled by British artillery, Percy's men ran a withering gauntlet, reaching their destination at sunset. For eighteen of the thirty miles, covered in eighteen hours, the British had been held to a running fight which had cost them nineteen officers and 250 other ranks killed and wounded. In the 47th five men had been killed and two officers and twenty-one men wounded. The grave at Lexington of several British soldiers, tended to this day, symbolizes in a small way the first severe skirmish of the war.

The next action in which the 47th was engaged was the ensuing Battle of Bunker's Hill where the ultimately victorious redcoats, steeped in the irrelevant tactics of Dettingen and Fontenoy, were nearly annihilated. It was to be an extravagant price to pay for what the Americans clinically call 'real estate'.

Immediately on their arrival the three major-generals were urged by Gage to take vigorous action. Gage proclaimed martial law and an amnesty, and laid down military plans which brought a vigorous reaction from the American Army. These plans had included the occupation of the Charlestown peninsula and the Dorchester Heights, overlooking Boston. But the Americans acted quickly (owing, it is said, to the lack of security by 'Gentleman Johnny' Burgoyne), and, on the night of 16–17 June, 1775, they occupied Bunker's Hill and Breed's Hill on the peninsula, but not without considerable commotion which fired Clinton with the desire to reoccupy the features.

The following order was issued at 10 am on 17 June:

The ten Eldest Companies of Grenadiers and the ten Eldest Companies of Light Infantry (exclusive of those Regiments lately landed), the 5th and 38th Regiments to parade at half after eleven o'clock with their arms, ammunition, blankets and provisions ordered to be cooked this morning. They will march by files to the Long Wharf. The 43rd and 52nd Regiments, with the remaining companies of Light Infantry and Grenadiers, to parade at the same time with the same directions, and to march to the

North Battery. The 47th Regiment and the 1st Battalion of Marines will also march as above directed to the North Battery after the rest are embarked and be ready to embark there when ordered . . .

Howe, the senior major-general, and a confessed admirer of the Americans' spirit, duly commanded the operation and Gage watched from rising ground twelve hundred yards away. At 1 pm the Grenadiers, Light Infantry, and the 5th, 38th, 43rd and 52nd Regiments landed at the eastern end of the Charlestown peninsula. At this moment Howe realized that his army had been supplied entirely with ammunition for 12-pounder guns, whilst he possessed only 6-pounders. His riflemen engaged the Colonists' sharpshooters at too great a distance, whilst they waited until his men were well within their range. Twice the redcoats, carrying loads of 125 lb each and advancing through waist-high grass in scorching weather, were led by Howe and twice they were forced to retire. But now, under Clinton's command, the 47th and the Marines landed further west and closed upon the southern flank of Breed's Hill. This time the Colonists, running severely short of ammunition, chose not to wait for the bayonet charge of the surviving redcoats who, having dumped their packs, were incensed by the loss of so many of their comrades. Now the Royalists swept over the hills, all along the line, and up to the Charlestown Neck, leaving behind 1,146 casualties out of a total strength of 2,500 men.

The 47th was detailed to control the entrance to Charlestown itself, and on 27 September the whole army involved received the thanks of the King for their gallantry and an order which, in effect, recalled Gage from Command and replaced him by Howe.

No regiment could have been more actively engaged in the American War of Independence than the 47th, for they were next involved in the northern sector against the American army under Montgomery and Arnold, which invaded Upper Canada and tried to capture Quebec. The Colonists had occupied Dorchester Heights on 6 March, 1776, and with the vastly disparate size of the rival armies (18,000 Americans and 6,646 British fit for duty) it was decided to withdraw and reinforce Carleton's Canadian garrison, in response to the Governor's appeal. The first regiments to reach him were the 47th, via Halifax, and the 29th (later the 1st Worcesters) from London. The 47th would now belong to the 1st Brigade (commanded by their own Col Nesbitt), together with the 9th (later The Royal Norfolks) and the 31st (later the 1st East Surreys).

This time the Americans were not so fortunate, and after the death of their commander, Gen Richard Montgomery, Arnold's force was beaten by Carleton, who did not make Montcalm's mistake of being enticed from the fortress of Quebec. But Carleton failed to follow up his success, and it was not until the following year that the projected march to Albany and New York began, by which time the initiative was lost.

Carleton, a fine soldier, was criticized at home for his failure to carry the advance southwards; and for the offensive of 1777 the command of the northern army passed to the brave, ambitious and urbane Burgoyne who was as much an authority on wine and beautiful women as on military matters. The campaign had originally been his idea although, in retrospect, one wonders how he could seriously have considered a strategy which created long lines of supply, daily more attenuated and vulnerable to attack by guerrilla forces, in such strange and hazardous country as the Hudson Valley. Now, largely because of the bungling of the operation by Lord George Germain,[1] the Colonial Secretary in London, there followed perhaps the worst disaster of the war, the news of which was the signal for French intervention on behalf of the American rebels. The plan was for Burgoyne's force to link up with that of Howe and Clinton, advancing northward from New York. But Germain's orders were never fully communicated to Howe, or perhaps the Commander-in-Chief disagreed with them because of his own preferred cam-

[1] After Germain's mysterious failure to lead his cavalry division into action at Minden, cowardice was alleged, but to clear his name he voluntarily underwent court-martial, as a result of which he was deemed unfit for further command. On leaving the Army he entered Parliament, and despite his record he managed to secure the joint portfolio of the secretaryship for War and the Colonies.

paign against Washington at Brandywine, a notable Royalist victory, and Philadelphia (which Germain also sanctioned). In the event, rumours of Clinton's advance reached Burgoyne in the last stages of the latter's melancholy thrust southward, and Burgoyne's plan to cut off the New England states from the interior was ground to a halt at Saratoga.

The advance began on 4 June, with the following regiments and corps taking part: the entire battalions of the 9th (later The Royal Norfolks), the 20th (The Lancashire Fusiliers), the 21st (The Royal Scots Fusiliers), the 24th (The South Wales Borderers), the 47th, the 53rd (the 1st K.S.L.I.) and the 62nd (The 1st Wiltshires). In addition were the flank companies of the 29th (the 1st Worcesters), the 31st (The 1st East Surreys) and the 34th (the 1st Border Regiment). There were also five hundred artillerymen, bringing the British total to 4,135. Swelling the ranks were 3,116 Germans (Hessians and Brunswickians), under Gen von Reidesel, and a force of Canadians and five hundred Red Indians, so that Burgoyne's army totalled just over 7,900 officers and men.

Leading the vanguard of the initial advance was Capt Craig of the 47th, whose name frequently occurs in histories of the war and who was wounded near Hubbarton on 7 July. Commanding four companies of Light Infantry he reached the Bouquet River on 10 June, while ten days later the whole army was concentrated at Cumberland Point at the northern end of Lake Champlain. All went well, particularly at the capture of Fort Ticonderoga where Major-Gen Phillips, a former artilleryman who commanded the brigade containing the 47th, captured Sugar Loaf Hill from which his guns could control the fort, obliging the rebels to retreat to Castleton, thirty miles to the southeast.

The first fierce resistance was at Fort Anne, near Skenesborough, where the army was concentrated on 10 July. Reinforcements of the 47th and 53rd regiments were here called up to assist the 9th before the garrison set fire to Fort Anne and retired to Fort Edward.

The next objective was the Hudson River itself, and here

Burgoyne made his first serious blunder. Given two alternative routes of approach, he took the more difficult since, although it involved the traverse of very rough country, it appeared to be a direct advance. The Army took twenty days to cover as many miles and arrived at Fort Edward on 30 July. The delay enabled the retreating rebels to regroup. Then came the second, and more serious, disaster when Burgoyne sent a raiding expedition to replenish supplies from Bennington. Here the men, hopelessly outnumbered, faced a newly recruited American brigade of 1,500 men and sustained 500 fatal casualties. Despite these losses, Burgoyne had to hive off various units to protect his lines of supply. The thousand men left at Ticonderoga included two companies of the 47th, whilst another detachment of the Regiment found the garrison at Fort George.

By 15 September the Hudson was crossed, the bridge destroyed and the advance continued along a relatively well defined road towards Albany, thirty miles away. Meanwhile, on 8 September, six thousand Americans, under their new commander Gen Horatio Gates (who had begun his military career as an ensign in the 20th Foot), took up entrenched positions on Bemis Heights. Arnold commanded another force on the left and advanced slightly, so that the entire rebel army in this sector amounted to 14,000 men. They now awaited Burgoyne's three columns, the left-hand of which consisted of the 47th (in charge of the boats) and the Germans, all under Reidesel's command. By this time Burgoyne had only five thousand men who, despite crippling losses at Freeman's Farm and Bemis Heights north of Stillwater, bravely moved in on 9 October to assault the Americans at Saratoga; but by the time Burgoyne realized reluctantly that withdrawal was his only course, a force of rebels had cut off his retreat. The British losses near Stillwater had been crippling, and Capt Craig was wounded for the third time during the advance.

The southern thrust never arrived. Morale was now desperately low among Burgoyne's men who had suffered not only constant deluges of rain, but, on one macabre occasion, the exposure by this inundation of the buried corpses of some of their comrades, with all the accompanying stench.

It is strange that Burgoyne, a man of original (if questionable) strategic ideas, was so dilatory in the execution of them. Even at the last moment Col Sutherland of the 47th told the General that speed in occupying the heights above Fish Creek beyond Saratoga would compensate to a large extent for the disparate size of the armies. But by now Burgoyne, who had never previously allowed thoughts of defeat to discourage him and for all his deficiencies had never lacked in courage, had lost the will to continue. He sent a deputation, which included Capt Craig, to arrange a convention with the rebels whereby Burgoyne hoped that, on condition that they would not return to the American Colonies, his men might be allowed home. This was agreed by the chivalrous Gates, but Washington, realizing that the presence of these men in Britain would enable fresh regiments to be released for the American war, declined to ratify the agreement. It was at Craig's suggestion that the word 'convention' was substituted for 'capitulation' in the original draft.

And so the 47th with the rest of Burgoyne's force remained in America, although many survivors returned to England after the Declaration of Independence and rejoined the Colours. By then, however, many other prisoners were too dispersed to regard themselves as anything but the disinherited forbears of a regiment that would rise again. Only recently, as evidence of the privation which the Regiment suffered at Saratoga, several bones and buttons (the latter firmly inscribed '47') were found in a shallow grave near Stillwater, long after the uniforms and their owners had decomposed into the earth of a foreign land.[2]

[2] Despite the several victories which they had won, no battle honours were accorded to those regiments of the British Army for their successful actions in the War of American Independence.

CHAPTER 4

The Loyal Lincoln Volunteers

THIS short chapter deals essentially with the junior battalion of The Loyal Regiment – the 81st Foot, or 'The
Loyal Lincoln Volunteers' – the corps which was eventually
to be paired with the 47th to form The Loyal North Lancashire
Regiment. The loyal men of Lincolnshire were, in due course, to
infuse fresh vigour into the stalwart men of Lancashire. But
before we turn to the raising of the 81st one important development must be mentioned.

Some veterans of the 47th returned home, in accordance with
the Convention, in November, 1781; whilst the less fortunate
prisoners were not released until the War of American Independence had ended in the recognition of the United States of
America at the Treaty of Versailles in 1783. Between these two
years the British Army had had a face-lift. The former draft was
sent to Lancaster and for the first time a connection was established between the British Army and the County of Lancaster,
resulting in the creation of The Lancashire Regiment. The second
draft returned to find itself also belonging to that regiment (but
now at Preston where the first depôt had been established), but
similarly with their numerical precedence as their essential identity. The reform of 1782 was the first step towards a settlement
of the British infantry on a county basis, which was to give it
the sense of identity that nourished it for more than a century
and three-quarters. But not until 1881 can we properly refer
to the regiments by their county names; and not until the old
Regular Army was decimated between August and December,
1914, did the unofficial use of the numerical system vanish from
British military life.

But to return to Lincoln: two other regiments, successively
disbanded, had previously been designated the 81st, but since
neither of them was a forbear of The Loyal Regiment it is irre-

levant to discuss them further. The one from which the Second Battalion, The Loyal North Lancashire Regiment evolved was raised by Col Albemarle Bertie, following a Royal Commission dated 23 September, 1793. This, of course, was in response to the call to increase the size of the run-down British Army, following the outbreak of the French Revolutionary Wars earlier that year.

The widening of Britain's scattered empire was absorbing her Army at an alarming rate (one wonders, in fact, how we would have managed had we still had the American Colonies). The Seven Years' War, which had ended thirty years earlier, had vastly increased British military responsibility, and whilst unbroken hostilities had been waged in the West Indies ever since, either with the natives or the French, the St Lawrence had had to be constantly garrisoned and men had been seconded to the East India Company to secure Clive's victories in the sub-continent. The third, and last, 81st had been born at a vital moment and in a most heartening manner.

But Bertie's regiment was initially the 83rd, and it so remained for a short time, whilst the 81st (the second of that number) and the 82nd, raised at the same time, struggled precariously before being forced into disbandment. Certainly, by 25 October, 1793, it was known as the 83rd, as witnessed by this advertisement, printed in *The Lincoln, Rutland and Stamford Mercury* on that day:

'Old England for Ever.
'Honour and Glory.
'A large bounty will be given to all Loyal Lincolnshire Volunteers, or 83rd new-raised Regiment, commanded by the Right Hon Major-General Albemarle Bertie, Colonel of The Lincolnshire Volunteers, and the Hon Lieut Colonel Lewes.

'Those Loyal Heroes, who, ambitious of gaining Glory in the Honorable Profession of Arms, have now an opportunity of entering a Regiment, where Honour and Happiness, will be sure to reward their noble exertions for their King and Country, and a liberal pension will soften the Sorrows of declining life, and procure a more comfortable competence than can be acquired by many years of hard labour. Every Hero will be provided with genteel clothing, fit for a Gentleman Soldier.

22

'Boys, five feet four inches high, under twenty years of age, and men, five feet five, above that age to thirty-five, will be accepted.

'The present moment calls for the exertion of all good subjects for a short period, and it is believed will be very short indeed.

'Young men of abilities will be preferred to Sergeants and Corporals by applying to the Commanding Officer, Headquarters, Lincoln: or to Sergeant-Major Fawkner, Stamford.

'Bringers of good recruits will be liberally rewarded.

'God Save the King.'

Evidently, in 1793, to be a 'gentleman' was as coveted an attainment as is that of a 'professional' today! This was the age when the social ravages of the Industrial Revolution were claiming their first victims, and when only the legacy of 'Turnip' Townshend – Lord Charles Townshend, under whose auspices agriculture was revolutionized in the Fenlands by the introduction of turnips as fodder for cattle during the winter – could bring any hope to the tens of thousands lingering below subsistence level in the Fenlands. Certainly such an enticing advertisement brought hope and inspiration to the men of Lincolnshire. It is recorded that when the call came the Militia of the County (including many men of very doubtful military experience) came forward as a body to serve in Bertie's new regiment, and henceforth they were popularly known as 'The Loyal Lincoln Volunteers', a title not officially adopted until 1832.

But there was more to it than that. The family motto of Albemarle Bertie, who subsequently succeeded to the marquisate of Lindsay and the dukedom of Ancaster, was *Loyauté M'Oblige*, a motto which passed through the 81st and, in 1934, was adopted by The Loyal Regiment.

CHAPTER 5

Napoleon is Taught a Lesson

THE loyal men of Lincolnshire suffered appallingly from yellow fever in the West Indies during the French Revolutionary and Napoleonic Wars; and were ill-rewarded when, after service in South Africa, they were sent to reinforce the 22nd Regiment (later the Cheshires) in India.

Napoleon's armies first crossed bayonets with the British at the Battle of Maida on 4 July, 1806. It was an occasion on which the Regiment particularly prided itself. The 1/81st Foot was the largest corps in a relatively small force, commanded by Major-Gen Sir John Stuart, which was to inflict the first defeat on Napoleon in Europe. The action developed into a furious hand-to-hand encounter which resulted in the Regiment's first battle honour, bringing some consolation for all the misfortune which the 81st had experienced in the Caribbean and South Africa.

After service in Jersey and Malta, when it seemed that action would once again be denied to it, the Regiment was part of a four-brigade force of 5,531 officers and men which was to be landed in Calabria, near the toe of Italy, by a fleet under Rear-Admiral Sir Sidney Smith, to encourage the Neapolitan guerrillas (the word 'guerrilla' was not, in fact, coined until Spanish civilians took up arms against Joseph Bonaparte in the Peninsula) in their struggle against Joseph Bonaparte who had been placed on the throne of Naples after its annexation by Napoleon early in 1806.

Part of the 81st was placed in the Advanced Corps, of approximately brigade strength, which was to be commanded by an unusually brave soldier, the Regiment's own Lt-Col James Kempt. Stuart commanded the British army which had recently been withdrawn to Sicily, whence the embarkation began in complete secrecy on the night of 25 June. Sir John Fortescue wrote of this security in the *History of the British Army*, Vol. 5,

'Not a soul had any idea of the object of the expedition except the General and two of his staff; and it must be said that this part of the proceedings was admirably managed.'

The force arrived at the Bay of St Euphemia on the evening of 30 June, and at dawn next day the first landings took place unopposed. But soon the Corsican Rangers of the Light Brigade made contact with three companies of a Polish battalion from the French post at Monteleone. The heavy surf impeded the operation, and the 2 and 3 July were further occupied with the task of landing stores and equipment. But by then Gen Reynier, commanding part of the Calabrian garrison, had knowledge of the expedition and began to move southward from Reggio. On the night of the 2nd/3rd he arrived at Maida, nearly ten miles northward along the coast from Stuart's landing point. Stuart, in turn, heard that the French were now encamped on the River Lamato and, accompanied by a small grenadier escort, he led a reconnaissance patrol into the hills to observe the enemy's movements. To almost the same place, a few moments later, came the unwitting Reynier and a cavalry escort to observe the British! The enemy's army consisted of 6,400 men, including 5,700 infantry, made up of one Swiss, two Polish and six French battalions; and although it must have been quite evident to Stuart that he was considerably outnumbered, he decided to attack the enemy at first light next day, 4 July. Batteries were deployed to defend the beach-head and the order was given to advance.

The decision certainly surprised the French who, immediately after Austerlitz, regarded as impudent any attempt so deliberately to engage their armies. The British advance along the shore, thence inland, was made in three columns, with Kempt on the right commanding the Advanced Brigade of Light Companies. In the centre was Major-Gen Acland's 2nd Brigade with the 81st, and on the left Lowry Cole, soon to win renown at the Battle of Albuera. Brig-Gen Oswald brought up the rear with three field guns. Soon the brigades advanced in echelon, Kempt still leading the vanguard.

Meanwhile, Reynier's army swept down the hill from Maida and wheeled left, leaving his right or seaward flank the weaker

part of his line. Kempt had to face the French left on the bank
of the Lamato. Whilst the Light Companies of the 20th (later
The Lancashire Fusiliers) and the 35th (later the 1st Royal
Sussex) of Kempt's brigade drew first blood, Acland sent the
78th Highlanders (later the 2nd Seaforths) and the rest of the
81st forward to prevent the seasoned French 42nd Regiment from
guarding the exposed left flank of the enemy. Following up,
Acland brushed with Polish and Swiss troops, but it was the 81st
who routed the Poles, whilst the 78th overcame the Swiss, and
Acland's victorious brigade would have driven the enemy off
had they been equipped with suitable cavalry and artillery.

Now it was Kempt's turn again. His men pressed on in line,
halted about a hundred yards short of the enemy and found themselves opposite the redoubtable 1st Légère on the French left.
Volleys were exchanged before the French fixed bayonets and
advanced *au pas de charge*. But now the lunatic and unimpressed
British doubled forward at the trail to meet them. Seeing that
his men were encumbered by their blankets, Kempt halted the
line so that these could be discarded. Misunderstanding the significance of this the Légère redoubled their efforts, but were
amazed when the British did not scatter before them. Instead,
their enemy fired well aimed volleys at the French and then, also
fixing bayonets, charged to meet them. Kempt recorded the
French shock on impact when

> 'at that appalling moment French enthusiasm sank before British
> intrepidity and the bloody shock of actual conflict with the
> bayonet; their battalions broke and fled; they were instantly over-
> taken amidst deafening shouts, and assailed with such fury that in
> a few minutes 700 dead lay on the spot and 1,000, including
> General Compère, were made prisoners. The 1st Brigade
> (Acland's) had now come up, and they broke and drove before
> them at the point of the bayonet the French 42nd Regiment and
> two battalions of Poles; they then paused and poured into them
> an incessant fire of musketry, inflicting immense loss on the
> enemy.'

Reynier now tried to counter-attack the British left where
Oswald's brigade came up from support to a position between
Acland's and Cole's, which was deployed towards the coast. So

sudden had been the move that many of Oswald's men, who had foolishly yielded before the blaze of the noon-day sun, now grabbed their muskets and doubled up to face the French, naked except for their bandoliers. No doubt the surprised French must have wondered what unorthodox tactics this indicated!

The situation might have been serious but for the sudden reinforcement of Cole's brigade by the main body of the 20th which had just been put ashore by Admiral Smith. But the last stage – the pursuit of the beaten French – might have been more successful. 'If', wrote Col Bunbury, the QMG, 'we had then a couple of hundred of good cavalry, we might probably have destroyed the enemy's army; but we could do little more with our jaded infantry. Our column continued to advance upon the enemy till he abandoned the plain of Maida and retreated rapidly up the valley (beneath the town of that name) through which runs the road to Cantazaro.' The exhausted British halted on the Maida-Nicastro road. Bunbury continues, 'By midday our soldiers were resting on their arms, gasping with heat and thirst, and watching through the dust, with disappointed eyes, the rapid retreat of the French column. Our ammunition was nearly spent; there was no water for the men, save for those on the right, and every step we might make in advance led us further from our supplies of every sort.'

The total French casualties were over 4,000, whilst the British lost only forty-four killed and 284 wounded, the majority in the Light Brigade and in those companies of the 81st which were in Kempt's Advanced Corps. Calabria was rid of the French but, being insufficiently equipped for further advance, and with the possibility of battle with Marshal Massena, the British could only withdraw again to Sicily.

Gen Stuart had this to say of the 78th and the 81st of Acland's Brigade:

Major-General Stuart finds himself incapable of expressing to the troops the sentiments excited in him by their brave and intrepid conduct in the late action of the 4th, in which they gained so signal a triumph over a boasting and insolent enemy . . . The 78th and 81st Regiments, which formed the Brigade of General Acland,

shared the first and severest part of the action with the Light
Infantry, whom they were ordered to support, and the gallantry
and good conduct of the Brigadier-General in fulfilling this duty
were most nobly seconded by the brave regiments under his
orders . . .

Kempt's memento was more personal. Soon after the landing
at St Euphemia a small tortoise wandered into his tent where it
provided an excellent short meal for the hungry Colonel and his
staff officers. Subsequently, Kempt had the shell mounted in
silver and he presented it as a snuff box to the officers of the 81st
Regiment, and it has so remained a treasured relic of the Loyals.
Maida was indeed significant. It was the finest amphibious
operation since Quebec, whilst the *Encyclopaedia Britannica*
claims, 'the campaign is a classic example of the use of sea power
to achieve local superiority through mobility and surprise'. But,
above all, the Battle of Maida broke the myth of the invincibility
of Napoleon's armies in Europe.
The 1/81st was among those battalions from Sicily which were
to carry the war into eastern Spain in 1812–13, and across to
Biarritz. In 1814 it was ordered to go to Canada as a result of
the war with the United States, but returned too late to see action
at Waterloo.

CHAPTER 6

With Moore at Corunna

THE first phase of British intervention in the Iberian peninsula against Napolon's armies was not wholly creditable.
In August, 1808 Sir Arthur Wellesley established himself
in Portugal with 13,500 men (the defence of Portugal being
Britain's sole declared objective at that stage of the war), and
there followed in rapid succession his great victories at Rolica
and Vimiero. The command then passed successively to Sir
Harry Burrard (for a brief twenty-four hours) and then to Sir
Hew Dalrymple, who had been Colonel of the 81st from August,
1797, to January, 1798, whereupon the ignominious Convention
of Cintra, drawn up on 30 August between Dalrymple and the
French Marshal Junot, allowed the French army peacefully to
evacuate Portugal with all its spoils and return home. The Convention infuriated Napoleon no less than the British Government,
and he vowed reoccupation. Even Wellesley's reputation, as
Dalrymple's subordinate, was unjustifiably tarnished by the stigma
of this timid concession.

But in October, 1808, the British command in Iberia went to
Sir John Moore, the hero of the Light Infantry, and perhaps the
most daring and resourceful soldier of his day; a man, moreover,
who, like Wolfe, Gordon, Roberts, Plumer and Montgomery,
established immediate rapport with the British public and the
ordinary soldier. His method of training at Shorncliffe Camp was
legendary. Napoleon's redoubled efforts to conquer Spain diverted
Moore's attention from Portugal, and rather than re-embark his
army from Corunna he led the bulk of it across the frontier
towards Madrid, whilst Sir David Baird's First Division was sent
from England during the first week of November and landed at
Corunna to strengthen Moore's army. Although these two outstanding generals were eventually obliged to evacuate the British
army from Corunna in one of the most famous rearguard actions

in history, the reputation of the British Army was thereby enormously enhanced. Their courage and skill had saved Spain from being immediately overrun by Napoleon who was never to return to the country after his brief personal intervention at the end of 1808.

Three battalions of the Loyals' forbears, the 2/47th, the 1/81st and the 2/81st, served at various stages in the Peninsular War. The last-named was formed, together with many other second battalions, in 1804 to deal with the Napoleonic threat. This was made manifest in Iberia by Napoleon's determination to occupy this territory in order to complete his Continental System – the blockade of Europe to British trade. After rather desultory service in Ireland the 2/81st, now in Sir David Baird's First Division, had the honour (scarcely appreciated at the time) to take part in that legendary campaign which was concluded at the Iberian 'Dunkirk'.

The 2/81st was disembarked at Corunna on 7 November, 1808, and, with the rest of Baird's division, immediately began to drive towards Madrid. Like Moore's, Baird's success depended largely upon the fortunes of the Spanish themselves – both their Army under the Marquis de la Romana and the guerrillas. By 23 November Baird's division had reached Astorga, 115 miles to the south-east. But now came the confusion inherent in poor communications. Moore had said that if Baird's cavalry was well up by 1 December he should advance from Astorga to Benevente. At this moment the Spanish suffered a severe defeat on the Ebro and were in retreat. Moore decided on an immediate withdrawal to Lisbon to defend Portugal, and ordered Baird to embark at Corunna and join him. But the Marquis de la Romana implored Baird not to desert Spain while his army was trying to steady the retreat; and within a few days Moore countermanded his previous order and told Baird to return to Astorga whilst he, Moore, would proceed 'bridle in hand, for if the bubble bursts and Madrid falls we shall have to run for it'. Baird was ordered to send his cavalry to Zamora and the rest of his force to Benevente. Moore heard of the fall of Madrid, but decided to strike Soult at Burgos.

Only from time to time does news of individual regiments break through. According to the diary of an officer in the 15th Hussars who breakfasted with officers of the 2/81st on 3 December, the battalion had evidently been covering Baird's retreat.

On the 10th the 2/81st, with the rest of the Division, was to join forces with Moore at Valladolid when a startling discovery changed the whole prospect. A message from Berthier (Napoleon's senior marshal) to Soult was intercepted by the British, and Moore learnt at once of the total strength and disposition of the enemy in the Peninsula. Soult was to seize Leon, Zamora and Benevente. Believing Moore to be *en route* to Lisbon, Berthier told Soult that his way was clear and that he should finally consolidate at Burgos.

Moore would now avoid the trap here and strike at the flank of the unsuspecting Soult. The whole British army was accordingly united on 20 January at Mayorga. The pay-roll of the 2/81st at this juncture recorded that only three private soldiers had been killed and that six were missing, whilst of those with the Colours, Fortescue wrote that they were 'in good health and order, their behaviour so far had been exemplary; and their confidence in themselves was, if anything, rather too great'. The total strength of Moore's army was 29,357, a considerable drop since embarkation at Falmouth. But now came news which could not fail to alarm even Moore and Baird. Just as the plan to attack Soult at Saldana on the Carrion River was about to be launched, with every promise of outstanding success, Moore told Baird to come and see him urgently; he had fresh information. The French were advancing northwards from Madrid, whilst moving fast from eastern Spain towards Benevente, and threatening to sever Moore from Baird, was Napoleon himself. To the great disappointment of the British soldiers the attack was called off and the 2/81st, like the other regiments, 'retired to their quarters in a state of sullen silence . . . We all rose next morning perfectly ignorant as to the fate which awaited us.' (Lord Londonerry, *Narrative of the Peninsular War*, Vol 1.) From this moment began the long withdrawal to the coast when Moore managed, by rare leadership, to minimize the difficulties emphasized by Wellington; 'Nothing is so unmanageable as a British army in retreat.'

The roads were washed away in many places during that terrible winter of 1808–9. Snow, rain and blizzards often scattered the hungry and demoralized men blindly across many square miles of desolate country. The snowdrifts on each side of the road were usually higher than the tips of the soldiers' fixed bayonets. Astorga was crowded out with three allied divisions, so that Baird had to march on and camp beyond the town. Dumps of clothing and other supplies, left on the outward march, had to be destroyed. On 30 December Baird's division reached the village of Torre in a blizzard, suffering from severe exhaustion – a state which weakened their resistance to the effects of the wine which they drank by the gallon when they broke open the cellars and casks in a state of uncontrollable frustration and anger. It was, as Lord Londonderry wrote, 'exceedingly difficult to rouse them' to continue the dreary retreat next morning. Many had to be left behind in their stupor, victims of the swords of the French dragoons or of the foul and infested prison camps. But nevertheless on New Year's Eve and the following day the First Division covered fifty miles in thirty-six hours. It is evident that Moore had in mind to use Baird's men to defend the harbour perimeter since they were regularly the first to leave for the day's march.

Moore had planned to hold the enemy at Lugo where, according to Fortescue, he had selected a position which was 'exceedingly strong'. But the realization that there was only one day's supply of bread left in Lugo, and the fear that Soult's army was about to be strengthened by a further corps under Ney, obliged Moore to carry on towards Corunna. Again, his men were bitterly disappointed. The destruction of the bridge over the Minho River severely impeded the pursuing French, but the British soon became so dispersed across the country that time had to be wasted whilst the stragglers caught up. One regiment entered Betanzos, twenty miles further on, with only nine officers, three sergeants and six privates; but the 2/81st held together remarkably well. After further delay the re-collected army proceeded on its way. Here the worst of the retreat ended, for on 11 January the weather improved and that night Moore entered Corunna. Soult's caution, Moore's harassment, the covering actions of Paget's division and the cavalry, the inclement weather – all had served to maintain a substantial lead for the bulk of the retreating British, and, satisfied that there was now no more chance for retreat, the men set about constructing the perimeter defence around Corunna with renewed vigour and optimism.

Moore had originally favoured withdrawal from Vigo, but on contrary advice he chose Corunna. About 5,000 men had been killed or taken prisoner, and 3,500 had already left from Vigo, with the result that only 15,000 men (all infantry except 200 gunners) remained behind to oppose Soult.

Hope's brigade was on the left of Moore's line, which extended from the estuary of the El Burgo River to the western end of the Monte Mero Ridge. Manningham's brigade, with the 2/81st in the centre, formed the right-centre. The weakness lay to the west of the village of Elvina where the ground fell sharply into a wide valley, leading straight towards Corunna, so that Moore's right could be turned. But the divisions of Paget and Fraser were staggered in reserve to cover this aperture.

Soult was prepared to wait for a week while Ney caught up, but when he saw the transports in the harbour he realized that time was short. The battle began early on 15 January, 1809.

The French soon occupied the crest of the ridge, and Soult tried to carry Elvina and turn the British right. Gen Merle (thirteen battalions) was to take the centre and another division (ten battalions) was to hold the left flank. Meanwhile, the French cavalry was to work around the British right and cut their line of retreat. Moore planned to start embarkation at 2 pm and to move the bulk of his army after dark. The main fight developed around Elvina where Baird was seriously wounded and evacuated from the field. Moore, on hand, ordered up two more rather depleted divisions. Meanwhile the musketry of those British who had held on to the Monte Mero Ridge was telling on the French, and two columns were repulsed by the British bayonet.

At this moment Sir John Moore, whilst riding from one hard pressed battalion to another, was knocked from his horse by a round shot which tore into his left breast and shoulder, exposing part of his upper lung. But still his thoughts were with the progress of the battle. Although his death was not to be at the very moment of victory, like those of Wolfe and Nelson, he had successfully conducted an operation infinitely more difficult than theirs. Charles Wolfe's famous poem, *The Burial of Sir John Moore at Corunna* ('We buried him darkly at the dead of night,/ The sods with our bayonets turning'), was incorrect in nearly every detail, but accurate in the spirit it evoked. With Moore's death, command devolved upon Sir John Hope.

Paget's reserve and Baird's division pushed back the encroaching French, whilst their second attack on Elvina had exhausted Merle's remaining reserve troops, so the French general brought up his last men. These troops had now to move across the ridge to the British right, in front of Manningham's brigade which was sent to take this column in the flank. The 3/1st (later The Royal Scots) and the 2/81st were now closely engaged, and after two hours' savage fighting on the gorse- and rock-covered ridge the 2/81st had sustained the loss of fourteen officers and about 140 other ranks, killed and wounded. When their ammunition was exhausted Hope sent for Leith's brigade, and Leith himself took the opportunity of complimenting the 2/81st for its gallantry in front of Corunna.

Indeed, as dusk fell, the French broke off the action. At 9 pm the embarkation continued, whilst only a few picquets watched the distant camp fires of the exhausted French. In his despatch of 16 January Hope wrote:

> On no occasion has the undaunted valour of the British troops ever been more manifest . . . the brunt of the action fell upon the 4th, 42nd, 50th and 81st Regiments, with part of the Brigade of Guards and the 26th Regiment.

In a General Order circulated from HMS *Audacious* off Corunna Hope recorded:

> Major-Gen Manningham with his brigade consisting of the Royals, the 26th and 81st Regiments will also be pleased to accept his best thanks for their steady and gallant conduct during the action.

The embarkation was completed on the afternoon of 17 January, 1809, the last ship leaving before sundown. The 2/81st, like most battalions, was split up in several battleships and transports. It is recorded that HMS *Victory* contained some of the Regiment's survivors – thirty officers, 291 other ranks, twenty-one women and one child. Oman gives the full embarkation strength of the battalion as 478 all ranks. Although the 2/81st had suffered few casualties in the early part of the campaign, its pre-eminence at Corunna had considerably raised the total, so that its loss of 241 all ranks during the battle was the highest in the brigade, and was exceeded in Baird's division only by the 264 lost by the 1/50th (later the 1st Royal West Kents). The 2/81st's total casualties in the campaign were fifteen officers and 311 other ranks. The survivors reached Plymouth on 28 January.

Corunna was the culmination of a long retreat, and Moore had managed the 'unmanageable'. But to the Loyals, as proud to have served under Moore as under Wolfe, the name was scarcely less resonant with glory than Quebec, Kimberley or, for that matter, Dunkirk. For this the Regiment earned the battle honour, 'Corunna'.

CHAPTER 7
The Ubiquitous Regiments

THE courageous but unfortunate veterans of Corunna were now sent on that ill-fated expedition to Walcheren, and the 2/81st suffered worse through disease there than any other British battalion. They were not to return to the continent of Europe again, and although the 81st missed Waterloo, General Kempt commanded the 5th Brigade there before taking over the mortally wounded Picton's 5th Division. Kempt was Colonel of the 81st from 1819 to 1829. The 2/81st was unceremoniously disbanded in 1816.

The 47th formed the Lancashire Regiment in 1782, and its second battalion represented it in the Peninsula where it struggled to hold Andaluzia until, advancing victoriously towards the Pyrenees, it was present at Vittoria, the decisive battle of the War. Victors at Toulouse, the battalion subsequently returned to England and was disbanded in March, 1814.

The 47th Regiment has an unusual story among its archives. Occasionally fathers who had long family ties with a regiment put their sons' names down at birth for a commission in that corps. In June, 1803, one John Harley joined the 47th as a quartermaster on transfer from the 54th (later the 2nd Dorsetshire Regiment), and in his book *The Veteran* he related how a certain Capt Maurice Farmer, only seventeen years old, who had joined the regiment at Colchester in October, 1803, was yet one of the most senior captains in the British Army, 'having obtained his commission while still in his cradle'. By the age of nine he had, *in absentia*, been granted a captaincy, so that when eventually he was considered old enough to join the Colours he had more than a head-start on his fellow officers. This was one of those anachronisms which would have been unthinkable in the post-Wellingtonian army.

It frequently happened that whilst the Army's second and third

regimental battalions (raised by the Additional Forces Act of
1803) were those devoted almost exclusively to the purpose for
which they were raised, namely the defeat of Napoleon (which
for the British Army was chiefly in the Peninsula), the original
army was that which, to a greater extent, was engaged elsewhere.
This is a paradox of emergency conscription and a notable
phenomenon of more recent wars.

In 1806–07 the 1/47th was part of that force which had so
ignominiously to withdraw from South America after a hare-
brained plan to break Spanish colonialism there. The Regiment
went thence to India.

During the Battalion's first tour of India it was engaged in
three widely scattered campaigns – against the Joasmi in Arabia,
the Mahrattas and Pindaris and the Burmese kingdom of Ava.
The era of policing the already acquired Empire (notably in
India) had arrived, and the 47th was there at the outset.

It was the old story of the world powers (a phenomenon which
had really only existed since the end of The Seven Years' War)
using the unwitting local peoples to fight their wars for them.
In this case, Russia (which has always been expert in this respect)
and France, briefly at peace after the Treaty of Tilsit in 1807,
were trying to undermine the increasing power of Britain with the
help of local subversive factions among peoples as diverse as the
Persians, Arabs and Afghans. Britain, adopting a familiar counterpoise, immediately responded by establishing formal diplomatic
relations with the governments of those minor kingdoms in order
to suppress their respective brigands.

The 47th, stationed in Bombay (whence it had recently been
active against Portuguese colonists in Goa and elsewhere) was
part of a force sent to suppress the Joasmi pirates at Ras-el-
Khyma on that promontory of Arabia which protrudes into the
Persian Gulf. The combined assault, at first light, on 13 November, 1809, by the 47th and 65th (later the 1st York and Lancaster)
was a classic amphibious operation, enticing the enemy from his
fortifications on the one side and then striking him from the
other. It was, in fact, an exercise in fire and movement long
before that famous tactic had been devised. Victory was swift

and decisive and, after further skirmishing, the 47th returned to
Bombay to face two considerably more difficult campaigns.

Meanwhile, very much in the tradition of prized British military expertise, apparent again recently in the Trucial States, an
officer of the 47th was retained by the Shah of Persia to train
his Army into an efficient fighting force. For this the officer concerned was presented by His Majesty with an especially be-
jewelled scimitar.

The Regiment remained in Bombay for the season 1810–11
where, again in collaboration with the 65th, it was called on to
restore order among the subjects of the Gaikwar of Baroda in
the Rann of Kutch. As in Persia, so in India the British were on
hand to uphold the established authority.

A new problem presented itself during the ensuing Mahratta
(or Pindari) War of 1817–18. Brigands of all castes and tribes,
organized in bands throughout southern and central India, waged
annual guerrilla warfare against each other. Now, for the first
time, they had also to contend with the British Army. The initial
death-toll and damage they caused in 1817 was enormous, until
the Governor-General, the Marquis of Hastings, decided to root
out the Pindaris, whatever the consequences. Against 106,000
Horse, 81,000 Foot and 589 guns he deployed the largest army
which was ever mustered in India, divided into the Grand Army
in the north and the Deccan or southern Army – the former
under Hastings and the latter under Lt-Gen Sir Thomas
Hyslop.

The Gujerat Division, under Maj-Gen Sir William Keir, was
part of the Deccan Army, ordered to protect Gujerat and prevent
a link-up with the Pindaris in the Deccan. The 47th was in the
1st Brigade of this Division, together with the 2/7th Native
Infantry, commanded by Lt-Col Elrington of the 47th. Part of
the Regiment, including Capt T. Backhouse (a son of Col Backhouse) who commanded the storming party, was the first in action
at the hill forts of Verampore and Kurjah on 22 and 27 October
in reply to disturbances in the northern districts of Gujerat. Again
the Regiment showed its swiftness, born of thorough training,
and there were no fatal casualties among its ranks – stronger

evidence of military efficiency than the frequently more glorious claim of heavy losses.

Responding first to one emergency and then to another, the Gujerat Division, particularly the hard fibre provided by the British 47th serving in an alien climate, covered extraordinary distances on foot with little evident reward for its toil. Suffice it to say that the most satisfying claim which Keir could make was that he had, by his dogged persistence, driven a particularly dangerous band of Pindaris into the hands of the waiting and merciless 17th Light Dragoons near Mandasor. Thereafter the Division was withdrawn for the defence of Gujerat and by the end of February, 1818, the power of the Pindaris was completely broken. On the disbandment of the Gujerat force the 47th remained in garrison at Baroda.

The ubiquitous Regiment was rather like the legendary Baron von Munchhausen who jumped on to his horse and rode off in all directions. Now came another short but very sharp tour of the Persian Gulf area. In 1819, the Bombay Government had decided finally to put down the recurring piracy in the Gulf, and a force of 1,645 Europeans and 1,424 Indians was prepared under Gen Keir's command. Again, the 47th and 65th comprised the British contingent, and although the latter is the only regiment in the British Army with the battle honour, 'Arabia', the Loyals might quite easily have been considered for a similar distinction. Capt Backhouse commanded the Light Companies at Ras-el-Khyma on 3 December, 1818, and next day Backhouse's order was 'to dislodge the enemy from a bank within 900 yards of the fort, which would serve as cover for the men and a depôt for the stores'. The Arabs were duly driven out and the 47th resisted sharp fire from the enemy all day, which eventually developed into an artillery exchange from only 300 yards.

The United Services Journal for 1829, having described the action, records the following:

> Major Molesworth, of the 47th, mounted the parapet of the trench to reconnoitre more minutely, and to ascertain how that formidable gun could be silenced. 'I see them loading it now', said he, 'now, now they are running it out. Look to yourselves my lads.'

In an instant he fell back into the trench, his head blown to atoms.

Keir was particularly commended for his work in subduing the Arabs, and prominent among other commendations for bravery were the names of Molesworth and Backhouse.

If the Burmese campaign was to prove trying to Gen Slim's famous Fourteenth Army (in which the 6th Loyals were proud to serve) in the Second World War, it may be imagined how uncomfortable were the conditions here for the ill-equipped British foot soldier well over a century earlier. The troubles in Burma, simmering for some time, came to a head in 1824. As in 1942, the British were motivated by threats to India, but this time from the Burmese themselves in the form of the Kingdom of Ava, the capital on the Irrawaddy, twenty-five miles downstream from Mandalay. The King's embargo in 1811 of all British ships lying off Rangoon was peacefully received, and whilst Britain was engaged with the Mahrattas and Pindaris, the King confused tolerance with weakness. Together with the Anglo-Indian army under the command of Gen Sir Arthur Campbell the 47th was despatched to Rangoon to show at last that the Indian tiger had teeth. From this detachment, including the 47th, Elrington emerges again to deal with the ubiquitous enemy who were everywhere trying to cut off the rear of the column. The progress of Campbell's advance (severely molested here and there, notably at the strong position of Donubyu where the Burmese leader, Bandula, had selected a well-entrenched position) would have been praised by Slim himself.

In the storming of this and other stockades the 47th proved its dash and training, and among the names of several officers and men of the Regiment cited for gallantry that of Capt (later Major) Backhouse emerges once again, as also does that of Col O'Donoghue, commanding one of the detachments. The dislodgement of a strong enemy force from Prome by troops under Campbell and Brig-Gen Cotton, advancing astride the river, again involved the principle of fire and movement (albeit crudely executed at this stage), and demonstrated that in this type of bush warfare, as in the Maori Wars, the British Army, assisted by its new rocket guns, was using tactics not perfected in Europe until after the First World War.

The campaign continued up to the Battle of Ava itself when a treaty was signed on 24 February, 1826. In a General Order of April, 1826, the Governor-General of India named various regiments, including the 47th, for 'unfeigned admiration', in that they had 'eminently displayed the virtues and sustained character of the British soldier'. In the *London Gazette* of 28 December, 1826, following the thanks to the expeditionary force of both Houses of Parliament, the name of the 47th Regiment was among those which received the battle honour, 'Ava'. The Regiment at last returned to England in 1830.

But whilst the 47th had served so widely in India, Burma and the Middle East, the record of the 81st also enhanced the Loyals' reputation as one of the widest serving regiments in the British Army. Following its return to England in 1817, the 81st was sent to Canada (1822), the West Indies, England again (1831), Gibraltar (1836), the West Indies again (1839), again to Canada in 1843, to England in 1847 and so home to Preston. Each posting brought with it the adventure and responsibility of an over-stretched Army in an expanding Empire.

CHAPTER 8

The Crimean War

DESPITE the travelling and adventure involved in visiting remote parts of the world (something which, generally speaking, has only recently become possible for the ordinary civilian) it might seem that the British Army was beginning to tire of its globe trotting. The life of the private soldier, wherever he was, was undoubtedly restricted. His essential purpose, after all, was to fight according to the discipline of his training rather than to spend his career mounting guard outside far-flung British residences and sounding bugle calls at sunset for the reassurance of colonial settlers. Although further short tours awaited the 47th in Gibraltar, Ireland and the West Indies (still disease-ridden), one major campaign would soon demand all the courage and skill of the officers and men of the Regiment.

In November, 1852, three officers and eight other ranks were sent from Ireland to represent the 47th at the funeral of the Duke of Wellington. '. . . as the tombstone closed over our revered protector for ever', wrote the *Morning Post* on 19 November, 'are things engraven on our brain, to be re-called at will, whilst memory holds her seat.' Wellington had died on the eve of a campaign that sorely needed a great commander.

Already, in 1844, Tsar Nicholas of Russia had visited England and had expressed a particular wish to inspect a line battalion, recently home from foreign service. The 47th was duly chosen. 'Though your Guards are noble looking troops', said the Tsar, 'I confess I look with more interest on the sort of soldiers who win the victories for you in India and China.' The Franco-Russian aspirations which the 47th had helped to destroy in India and the Middle East gave His Imperial Majesty's words particular poignancy. But more ironical still was the fact that his audience was to play a distinguished part in curbing Russia's direct ambitions in the Balkans by the Anglo-French offensive in the Crimea only a decade later.

The causes of the Crimean War are too well-known to need much repetition here. It was calculated that Russia's designs to thrust at Constantinople (already indicated by her aggression in the Turkish Balkans) in order to gain entry to the Mediterranean would be launched from her great naval base at Sevastopol in the Crimea, and without waiting for events to reach that imminent stage the Anglo-French armies and the already involved Turks landed on the peninsula. All the ensuing battles were fought towards the gradually invested fortress of Sevastopol, and in all, except Balaclava (the cavalryman's battle), the 47th took a major rôle, and was proud to be granted three hard won battle honours in the bitterly fought campaign.

Initially under the command of the young Major Richard Farren – later Gen Sir Richard Farren, GCB, Colonel of the Loyal North Lancashire Regiment, 1885–1909 – the Regiment landed at Scutari, where the base hospital of the legendary Florence Nightingale was established, on 19 April, 1854. Belonging to Sir de Lacy Evans's Second Division the 47th shared the 2nd Brigade with the 41st (later the 1st Welch Regiment) and the 49th (later the 1st Royal Berkshire Regiment) under Brig-Gen H. W. Adams. Among a greatly increased regimental establishment it is interesting to note the addition of what was called a 'schoolmaster sergeant'. From Scutari they marched to Varna and embarked thence for a point six miles north of the Bulganek River, itself of equal distance north of the Alma.

As he watched the Second Division embark, that doyen of war correspondents, the great W. H. Russell of *The Times*, wrote,

'On Thursday last' – 31 August, 1854 – 'the 2nd Division embarked in excellent order . . . The 1st Brigade – 30th, 55th and 59th Regiments – and the 2nd Brigade – 41st, 47th and 49th – constitute a very fine division, which has suffered less from sickness than any other division in our army. They moved with great regularity down to the rude piers, and embarking, regiment after regiment, on board the steamers, were soon on board their respective transports.'

The French moved on the right or seaward flank and the British inland, the Second Division at the head of the rear column. In the southward advance from the Bulganek, which began on 19 September, the armies' first great engagement was on the Alma. The Second Division had now moved up to the right, next to the French who, it was wrongly expected, would bear the brunt of the strongly fortified enemy positions. The British Army consisted of 28,000 men and sixty guns and the French of 37,000 men and sixty-eight guns, supported by the fire of nine allied warships, whilst the Russians had well deployed only 13,000 men and thirty-six guns. The French were confronted with difficult and precipitous ground which was sparsely defended, and the British with a gentle grass slope of well entrenched positions. What faced the British at some distance has been graphically described by a famous eyewitness (Kinglake, *Invasion of the Crimea*, vol II):

> Those having good sight could detect on the slope across the stream something which looked like a brown seam, and, also numbering small black squares and oblongs on the green turf of the hillside. The brown seam was the Great Redoubt and the squares and oblongs were the columns of a Russian army.

The British suffered the initial disadvantage of being too closely grouped as they advanced in a 'thin red line', and the Second Division in its advance on the village of Bourliouk found its deployment restricted by the Light Division on its left and the French. Nevertheless, despite concentrated enemy artillery fire from Kourgane Hill, over the Alma on the left front, Lord Raglan, the British Commander-in-Chief, ordered an advance towards the ford, and a staff officer of the Second Division wrote: 'I shall never forget the excited look of delight on every face when I gave the order – "the line will advance" '. When the 41st and 49th had crossed the ford, the 47th effected a difficult crossing four hundred yards upstream, opposite the Russian left, and was thus able to gain a good position on higher ground from which to enfilade the obstructing Russians on Kourgane Hill. This enabled other British divisions to cross the Alma, and by 3.30 pm on 20 September, 1854, the enemy, having lost tactical advantage, was in full retreat.

The British casualties on the Alma were 2,002, the French 1,343 and the Russians nearly 6,000. Of the 47th one sergeant and three other ranks were killed; and four officers, four sergeants and fifty-seven men wounded. Among the dead, the sergeant and a corporal (both of the Colour Party) were killed when a plunging shot passed through the Queen's Colour.

Among the major battles of the Crimea there now followed the heroic Battle of Balaclava which was essentially a cavalry-man's battle. The allies desperately needed that port and threw in the Heavy and Light brigades. Had the successive French commanders, Saint Arnands (who, like Raglan, died of cholera during the campaign) and Conroberts not disagreed, Raglan would have struck straight at Sevastopol, but the circuitous route protracted the war and forced upon the British the cavalry losses at Balaclava and what became known as 'the soldiers' battle' at Inkerman on 5 November.

Inkerman was the culmination of the enemy's attempt to push the Allies from the peninsula. Menshikov, the Russian commander, had 115,000 men under command, and of the Allies' 65,000 men 16,000 were British infantry. The Second Division took the full force of the stealthy assault through the early morning mists. One enemy force was to prevent supplies being sent through from Balaclava, whilst two others were to converge upon the unsuspecting Second Division. The attack was supported by artillery from Shell Hill further west.

The picquets of the 41st, 47th, 49th and 55th (later the 2nd Border Regiment) regiments, caught unaware, had to act on their own initiative, and the poor visibility made it a soldiers' rather than a generals' battle.

Lt-Col Haly of the 47th, advancing as far as he could, ordered the Light Company to charge, and galloping at the first body of Russians he cut them down before he was unhorsed. Seeing him severely wounded and lying in the open, Capt Rowlands, 41st, and Ptes Kelly and McDermond, 47th, came forward to his

. Gen Sir John Mordaunt

2. Col John Hale

An old print of the Battle of Quebec, showing the British scaling the Heights of Abraham

4. Gen Albemarle Bertie

5. Major-Gen Sir James Kempt

6. The Battle of Maida on 4 July, 1806—it was the first occasion on which a French Army of the Napoleonic Empire was beaten in Europe

rescue. Kelly was killed almost immediately, but Rowlands and McDermond, in saving the Colonel's life, were subsequently awarded the Victoria Cross. Their names were among the first citations for the VC to appear in *The London Gazette* on 24 February, 1857, and they took part in Queen Victoria's first investiture parade on 26 June of that year.

The heroism of the picquets gave the rear echelons time to prepare, and it was not long before companies of the 47th, notably under Majors Fordyce and Farren, were deployed in line and, confronting the Russians with accurate fire, misled the enemy as to their strength. By the time certain units of the division were beginning to fall back before the Russians, reinforcements had arrived, and when elements of the leading 77th (later the 2nd Middlesex Regiment) joined with four companies of the 47th under Farren the enemy retreated, suffering the loss of many guns and the death of Gen Soimonoff, a leading architect of the battle. French support, sent by Gen Bosquet, ensured final success and the battle was virtually over by 1.30 pm. The losses were appalling. Of the 7,664 men of the Second Division present on Inkerman Ridge, 2,357 were killed or wounded. Of the 47th nineteen other ranks were killed, and two officers and forty-five other ranks wounded. Among the dead at Inkerman was Brig-Gen Adams himself.

The allies were slowly closing on the beleaguered fortress of Sevastopol. But the chief enemy now was the weather, and on 14 November a sudden blizzard presaged the onset of a ghastly winter which reduced the fighting strength of the Allies by half. Of the blizzard an officer of the 47th wrote,

'Our tents were lifted over our heads and the poles broken . . . the sick were obliged to wander about to find shelter where they could; many of them died a few days after.'

Twenty-one British ships were wrecked off Balaclava. For the victims of cholera and war, vital medical supplies were lost as were ten million rounds of ammunition, mostly for the newly adopted and very accurate Minié rifle. Then came the winter itself, of which Russell wrote,

C

'The condition of our army was indeed miserable, pitiable, heart-rending. No boots, no greatcoats – officers in tatters and rabbit skins, men in bread bags and rags; no medicine, no shelter; toiling in mud and snow week after week, exposed in open trenches or in torn tents to the pitiless storms of a Crimean winter ...'

On 6 January, 1855, it was announced that the strength of the 47th would be raised to 2,218 of all ranks, but by the end of March, due to disease and the weather, only 631 men were fit for action. During the spring, however, the Allies were strengthened particularly by French reinforcements.

The 47th was represented by eight officers and 300 men (with 600 more in support) at the assault on the Redan Redoubt on 18 June, 1855, when the Russians strongly resisted an artillery bombardment 'tremendous beyond all precedent' (Russell). Attack was followed by counter-attack, and the Redan battle dragged on with terrible losses on both sides. It was the Russians' most dogged defence of the war. When ammunition was nearly spent Colour Sgt McDonald of the 47th advanced over open ground to fetch a keg, returning with it under heavy fire of grape, shell and musketry. Nearly lost in oblivion now is the gallantry of Cpl Quinn, 47th, who, 'uttering an exclamation' as we are told, rushed a troublesome Russian rifle pit, killing an officer and four men and returning with a prisoner, saying that 'there are plenty more where he came from!' Quinn was conse-quently promoted to an ensigncy in the Regiment, without purchase.

The closing stages of the siege of Sevastopol began on 8 September and were marked particularly by the gallantry of the French who captured the Redan where the exhausted British had been repulsed. The 47th, like most of the Second Division, was not present at the final assault which met only diminished Russian resistance.

Peace did not come until the spring. Meanwhile, a static winter was remembered by the officers of the 47th chiefly for the opportunity to entertain the officers of the French 47th Regiment. Concessions from the Russians not to assault Constantinople were duly obtained by the Allies, but it had been at terrible cost to both sides. Into the names of the 47th's battle honours, 'Alma', 'Inkerman' and 'Sevastopol', is woven a tradition of courage and endurance which have become part of British military lore.

CHAPTER 9

India

MEANWHILE, it was now the turn of the 81st to assist in maintaining order in Britain's most cherished possession, still under the authority of the East India Company. Hardly had the Crimean War ended than the great Indian Mutiny broke out at Meerut on 10 May, 1857, and it found the 81st (the proud possessors of new Colours), who had arrived in India five years earlier, up at Lahore, the capital of the Punjab.

Without underestimating the glorious deeds of those regiments at the core of the Mutiny – at Meerut, Delhi, Lucknow and Cawnpore – it is frequently not appreciated what a vital part was played by the regiments which (in some cases barely in time) managed to disarm other threatening sepoys and check the spreading mutiny. Nowhere was this more vital than on the North-West Frontier and in the Punjab where the Russian-inspired Afghans and the Sikhs, who had fought a bloody war with Britain only a decade earlier, would have rejoiced at such military subversion. Of the one regiment of British cavalry and ten of British infantry stationed in the Punjab at the beginning of 1857, the 81st alone was in the capital.

News was quick to reach Lahore which had heard of the mutiny at Meerut via the 'bush telegraph' the next morning. On 12 May, however, came the official despatch from Delhi: 'We must leave office; all the bungalows are being burned by the sepoys from Meerut; they came in this morning; we hear that nine Europeans are killed.' And soon afterwards: 'Many native troops are in open mutiny, cantonments south of Mall burned; European troops under arms defending barracks; several European officers killed; electric telegraph wires cut.'

Brig-Gen Corbett, commanding the Lahore District, said that 'if anything is to be done, I will draw their teeth at once, and take their muskets'. At 4 am on 13 May, five companies of the

81st, with extra ammunition issued to every rather puzzled man, were drawn up on the huge parade ground at Mian Mir, opposite the distant ranks of the unsuspecting sepoys. With the Europeans were twelve guns, and after the Brigadier had praised the 81st for their distinguished services in the past and told them of the mutiny at Meerut, an order was given whereby the men fell back by numbers, to reveal the guns, followed by the snapped command, '81st, load!' The sepoys found themselves staring incredulously down the throats of the cannons, whilst on their flanks other companies of the 81st arrived, under Lt-Col Smith, to hold them in check. One historian of the scene, Bosworth Smith, wrote in *The Indian Mutiny*, vol 2.

> There was, it is said, a slight hesitation, but the ringing of the ramrods as the charges were rammed home, spoke eloquently in favour of obedience, and so some 2,000 muskets, and some 700 sabres soon lay piled on the ground. The extremity of the peril was now over, and the capital of the Punjab, with its 100,000 inhabitants, its cantonments, and its civil station was safe from the mutineers.

Spasmodic troubles persisted in the Punjab, but the efficiency and swift obedience of the 81st was the decisive factor which saved Lahore, and brought from Sir John Lawrence, the Chief Commissioner of the Punjab, a letter to Lt-Col Renny, commanding the 81st, in which he wrote,

> During the whole period of the crisis the consistency, endurance and good discipline evidenced by Her Majesty's 81st Regiment, were highly honourable to both officers and men. Could the corps have been spared it would have been sent to Delhi, but this was impossible; on it devolved the less glorious, but more irksome and equally important task of guarding day and night against the dangers which threatened us on all sides.

The last campaign of the 81st before its identity was lost under the Cardwell Reforms of 1881 was again in India. After service at home and in Gibraltar the Regiment was on the North-West Frontier during the Second Afghan War. At the root of this was Britain's suspicion of Russia's motives in Afghanistan and what these portended for India. The reception by the

Afghan ruler, Shere Ali, of a Russian mission at Kabul and his refusal to receive a British one, contrary to previous Afghan undertakings, led directly to the war of 1878–79. On 21 November, 1878, the three great passes leading into Afghanistan were entered by British forces, and on that day the 81st was involved in the fierce encounter at Ali Masjid, a heavily fortified position over the Khyber Pass which is particularly narrow at this point.

The clever deployment of the Anglo-Indian army under Gen Haines, the Commander-in-Chief in India, had managed to confuse the Afghans as to its movements, so that in the absence of a formal undertaking of compliance by Shere Ali the army was well placed.[1] The 81st, together with the 14th Sikhs and the 27th Punjab Infantry, constituted the 3rd Infantry Brigade. The 1st and 2nd Brigades were to work around to the rear of the fort, to positions commanding the enemy's anticipated direction of retreat. Meanwhile, the 4th Brigade attacked the right front.

At 9.30 am on 21 November, the 81st fired the first shots on an advanced and unsuspecting Afghan picquet. The allies had virtually invested the fortress, and by the time the 51st Regiment (later the 1st KOYLI) was sent to support the 81st, and artillery was brought down on Ali Masjid the next day, it was discovered that most of the elusive Afghans had, in fact, managed to slip away. Nevertheless, the main obstacle was brilliantly taken and the Anglo-Indian army was able to hold the strategic advantage from which, by the following spring, the British were able to exact the terms needed to end the war satisfactorily. From this campaign the 81st was awarded the battle honour, 'Ali Masjid' and 'Afghanistan, 1878–79'.

[1] The commander of the actual operation and of the Peshawar Field Force was Lt-Gen Sir Samuel Browne, VC, the originator of the officers' belt, named after him.

CHAPTER 10

The Defence of Kimberley

THE last quarter of the nineteenth century was a period of great change in the British Army. The reorganization brought about by Cardwell and his colleagues was more furiously debated and criticized in the clubs and messes of the day than even those which virtually abolished the regimental system in more recent times. The centre of military gravity had moved from the North-West Frontier to Whitehall.

This development, no doubt mentioned in every infantry history in this series, will be familiar to many readers. In 1873 all regiments above the 25th Foot (which, by their seniority, were allowed to keep their separate identity) were paired for alternate tours of home and overseas service – the former largely for recruitment and the latter particularly for India. The eight years which separated this from the major reform of 1881 may be equated with the same length of time between the disbandment or amalgamation of the old county regiments into Divisions of the Infantry today. The Loyals of course, avoiding amalgamation until 1970, was one of the last regiments to disappear. In 1881 Cardwell brought his reforms to their logical conclusion by replacing the old numerical precedence with county titles and in many cases scrapping the names which had been adopted in 1782. Thus the 47th Foot (The Lancashire Regiment) and the 81st Foot (The Loyal Lincoln Volunteers, as they were known from 1832 onwards) became respectively the 1st and 2nd Battalions, The Loyal North Lancashire Regiment. Many officers of the old line regiments resigned their commissions rather than be associated with this appalling system of regimental hybrid! But, fortunately for Britain in the wars which lay ahead, there was to be a gradual development of the volunteer and militia corps, later to be merged into the new regimental system and to win their spurs particularly in the Boer War where The Loyal North Lancashire Regiment won unique distinction. Although the Regiment was henceforth to be wholly associated with Lancashire, the regimental badge, until the Regiment's demise in 1970, was to incorporate the Red Rose of Lancaster with the Coat-of-Arms of the City of Lincoln, the latter forming the Loyals' collar badge.

Under their new title, the 1st Battalion arrived at Gibraltar from Preston in 1882, and two years later embarked for India where part of the Battalion was detached for the dangerous Zhob Valley operation in Afghanistan. Then followed twelve years of imperial policing, training and maintenance of internal security – tough, skilful and unrewarding work in some of the roughest country in the world. The Battalion moved to Cyprus in 1896.

Meanwhile, the 2nd Battalion returned from India in 1883 and, according to the new regimental policy, was stationed in Preston for eighteen months in 1895–97. With the Boer War imminent it sailed in 1899 for Malta, where it provided drafts and mounted infantry for service with the 1st Battalion in South Africa. But whilst the British Empire, now in its heyday, encompassed territories of absurdly disparate size, a detachment of the Battalion was sent to watch over the island of Cyprus, administered by Britain since 1878. Thence, with that extraordinary ubiquity to which the Army was well accustomed, it moved to Crete in 1900, Gibraltar in 1902, South Africa in 1904, Mauritius in 1907 and India in 1909. The outbreak of the First World War found the 2nd Loyal North Lancashires at Bangalore. But before 1914 plunged the world into that Armageddon from which it has never really emerged and the British Army into its first preoccupation with Western Europe for a century, the 1st Battalion had to fight perhaps the last of its great imperial engagements, on the South African veldt, from which it returned with a sense of achievement, albeit of severe reappraisal.

Whilst in Ceylon, actually on 1 June, 1898, the Battalion had acquired a new Commanding Officer transferred from The

Inniskillings, Lt-Col R. G. Kekewich, who became such a legendary figure during the Boer War that even in a recent television series, *The Regiment*, he was, apart from Kitchener, the only real military figure whom the BBC felt bound to portray in an otherwise fictional story. Kekewich was to Kimberley as Baden-Powell was to Mafeking and White to Ladysmith; and his Battalion earned a battle honour unique in the British Army, 'The Defence of Kimberley', the 1st Loyal North Lancashires being the only regular infantry battalion within that invested fortress. And locked up with them in the diamond mining town was the man to whose aspirations the war could perhaps be attributed – the Imperial colossus, Cecil Rhodes himself. But how was it that the Battalion found itself in this peculiar position?

The siege of Kimberley was the first of the three famous sieges of the Boer War (Kimberley, Ladysmith and Mafeking) on which the enemy based their strategy, and in view of the booty that lay within, and the paucity of the defending garrison, it was the most remarkable. Here was the mining Mecca of South Africa, and its founder, Cecil Rhodes, did not desert it during those dark months; in fact, he managed to reach the town just before the Boer ultimatum for investment expired on 11 October, 1899, with the Kimberley Light Horse, some five hundred strong, which he had rapidly and personally raised and horsed. From the first, Rhodes and Kekewich struck up a harmonious relationship, and throughout the four-month long siege the soldier and the Imperial visionary were to share and discuss their plans for bringing relief to the community for which they were, in their separate ways, jointly responsible.

The causes of the war are well known. Since the ill-fated Jameson Raid the Boers had not trusted the British denial of suzerainty over the Transvaal and the Orange Free State, and were suspicious of British designs on Cape Province and Natal. The situation deteriorated during the summer of 1899, and Britain's rejection in September of the Boers' claim that the Transvaal should become a sovereign state and the Boers' rejection of Britain's counter-proposals, led to war. The British

Army at home, including in Ireland and India, was put on alert
and President Kruger sent Britain an ultimatum to be considered
between 9 and 11 October for the recognition of Boer self-
government. On this not being met, Boer troops were despatched
to the Cape from the north and west. Fighting broke out on two
fronts about four hundred miles apart – at Mafeking, Kimberley
and the Modder River in the west, and at Colenso, Ladysmith
and the Tugela River in the east. The Loyals were on the former
front.

The 1st Loyal North Lancashire Regiment was one of the few
regular infantry battalions which had been stationed in South
Africa before the war, and it is evidence of the high regard in
which it was held that it should have been sent at once to the
town which was commercially valued above all others in the
Cape – Kimberley. Kekewich was ordered to keep open the lines
of communication with Mafeking to the north and the Orange
River southward. To defend Kimberley he anticipated war, now
only three weeks away, and sent an urgent cable to Cape Town,
requesting the following units:

	Officers	Other Ranks
23rd Company, RGA		
(with six 25-inch RML guns on mounted		
carriages)	3	90
7th Company, RE	1	50
Headquarters and four companies, 1st Loyal		
North Lancashire Regiment	9	413
Detachment, Army Service Corps	1	5
Detachment, RAMC	1	5
	15	563

On 20 September his requisition duly arrived. To Kimberley
itself went A, B, G and H Companies of the North Lancashires,
whilst on 21 September C, D, E, and F Companies went to the
Orange River Station further south.

On the whole, the main workings and buildings of Kimberley
favoured the defenders. An unobtrusive view could be held over

the surrounding flat country except to the west where, from Carter's Ridge, artillery fire could be brought down on the township from a distance of 4,000 yards. Barbed wire and arc lights, already installed by De Beers around the mounds which marked the disposition of the diamond digs, were an obvious advantage to Kekewich. Certain mounds, however, were only of doubtful value since their necessary occupation caused the defending forces to be unduly stretched, away from the centre of Kimberley.

Local volunteers were immediately available, and within a week over a thousand officers and men had been enrolled. These were soon to be needed by Kekewich, as the movement of the Boers of the Orange Free State, reported to be taking place opposite the Griqualand West frontier with the Cape Colony, indicated an early attack on Kimberley, and by 7 October the defences were virtually impregnable. According to *The Official History of the War in South Africa*, Vol. II,

'The Kimberley defences consisted of a series of redoubts with open gorges, which completely encircled the whole town and included Kimberley and De Beers mines. A part of the front of the *enceinte* was protected by barbed wire and abattis, and efforts were made to restrict egress and ingress to points on certain roads at which movable barriers had been erected. A series of advanced works to the south-east guarded Beaconsfield; Kenilworth formed a salient projecting northward; the Premier Mine was held as a detached post. An isolated redoubt on the southern road near Van Druyten's Farm and another to the westward of the town covering Otto Kopje's Mine completed the defences.'

Such was Kekewich's plan. The 48,000 white and coloured inhabitants, including 12,000 women and 10,000 children, had not long to wait for the first action.

The day after the ultimatum had expired the enemy destroyed the railway near Kraaipan, capturing an armoured train which was taking two guns to Mafeking and breaking telegraphic communications north and south. Kekewich sent a unit of his battalion, under 2/Lt Webster, to discover the point where the southern and more important raid had taken place, but at

Spyfontein Railway Station the party was completely outgunned by Boer riflemen to the south-east and had to withdraw.

On 15 October Col Kekewich proclaimed martial law in Kimberley and assumed supreme control of the civilian population – which presumably included its most famous citizen. The 1st Loyal North Lancashires and the Police were immediately deployed by companies and detachments, while Rhodes's mounted troops were invaluable in the task of pursuing raiders and capturing prisoners for the priceless information they yielded.

Leading the spearhead to relieve Kimberley was the First Division commanded by Major-Gen Lord Methuen, in the vanguard of which was the 9th Brigade. Kekewich used surprise tactics to clear enemy snipers from vital stretches of railway. He also aimed to draw off the enemy from the direction of Carter's Ridge and away from Lord Methuen's advancing troops. One foray led to the hostile force being rushed with the bayonet, and to the capture of nine wounded and twenty-four unwounded prisoners. In a later despatch of 15 February, 1900 (two days before the relief of Kimberley), Kewewich wrote:

> It will be observed that portions of the mounted corps were employed on every occasion. The work which fell on the Loyal North Lancashire Regiment, Cape Police, Diamond Field Horse and Kimberley Light Horse was in consequence very arduous; not only did the corps mentioned respond cheerfully, but nothing can exceed the bravery and dash with which these troops attacked the enemy on several occasions in his entrenched position.

This was the spirit of the resistance. Despite heavy Boer artillery ('Long Cecil', the monstrous gun of the defenders, was unfortunately deployed to cover the less important northward sector) the civilian morale remained high. Detachments of The Loyal North Lancashire Regiment used to lie out at night with the object of reducing the enemy's heaviest artillery by stealthy and decidely uncharitable fighting patrols aimed at the gun crews.

The 9th Brigade made first contact with a wing of the besieged garrison and most of the battle was to take place between

Methuen and Cronje, and his subordinate De La Rey, whilst other regiments were moved up to support the British against further enemy thrusts on the North Lancashires' still tenuous position at Kimberley. But this British success had not been achieved easily. By the middle of December the Boers had made a firm and successful stand to separate Kekewich from the 9th Brigade, by occupying a mile long stretch of Magersfontein Hill which commanded British positions between the Modder River and the vital railway northward to Kimberley. The garrison had been cut off once again, but after a 'Black Week' here, no less than at Colenso, reinforcements began to move to the Modder River, and the strengthened companies of the North Lancashires south of Kimberley (among whom Major Churchward had shown conspicuous bravery), together with the revitalized 9th Brigade, achieved the final breakthrough on 17 February. Two very mobile and lightly-armed cavalry brigades under Brig-Gen French (later to command the BEF in 1914) relieved Kimberley that day. The new Commander-in-Chief, Lord Roberts, was indebted particularly to The Loyal North Lancashire Regiment and their outstanding commander for the swift change of fortune that had made him a military legend.

The Regiment, both regulars and volunteers, were to be involved in further important operations in the Transvaal, particularly in the Western Transvaal where A and H Companies succeeded in dislodging a company of Boers from a rocky ravine at Haartbeesfontein. For this they received Lord Methuen's congratulations, and were presented with the flag they had captured. Throughout the war the 1st Loyal North Lancashire Regiment had marched over 4,500 miles, but it is by the great siege that the Regiment is best remembered; and for its outstanding conduct it was awarded a battle honour unique in the British Army – 'The Defence of Kimberley'.

On 6 October, 1904 a granite obelisk, twenty-five feet high, was unveiled by Major-Gen Kekewich to commemorate those members of the Regiment who had lost their lives in South Africa between 1899 and 1902. On it are recorded the names of seven officers and 117 NCOs and men. To the citizens of Preston

58

it is still a constant reminder of the distinguished part their own
Regiment played in that trying campaign.[2]

[2] It is an interesting coincidence that the 81st Foot should have
served in South Africa between 1799 and 1802, and a Loyal Battalion,
the 1st Loyal North Lancashires, between 1899 and 1902.

CHAPTER 11

The First World War

I<small>T</small> has been said, with heroic understatement, that the British
Tommy beat 'Kaiser Bill' with fags and tea. But the image is
correct. It conjures up the picture of exhausted and wounded
men at clearing stations, prone on stretchers, having given their
utmost (and too often their limbs), perhaps awaiting their return
to dear old 'Blighty' and sustained by cigarettes; or of those two
priceless ingredients holding morale together in the rat-infested
and waterlogged trenches near Ypres, on the Somme or at any
of those other notorious places which have passed into legend.
Here, as in nearly every other theatre of war, the Loyal North
Lancashires gave their blood and deepened their reputation as
a great regiment.

The Loyals provided twenty-one battalions, including three
of the 4th, four of the 5th and two of the 12th (territorials).
Kitchener's disinclination to use Haldane's Territorial Army
for overseas service until later in the War meant that these
territorial battalions arrived later in France, whilst one from
each parent battalion was reserved for recruitment at home. Yet
Kitchener's Army, famed for its recruiting poster, was thrown
into the inferno as soon as possible. As in most regiments, these
consisted of the middle and higher numbered battalions, known
as 'service battalions'. These began to arrive on the Western
Front in June, 1915, and whilst they soon established a great
reputation at Loos in September, it was by the battles of the
Somme, which began on that terrible first day of July, 1916, and
at Passchendaele, during the Third Battle of Ypres, particularly
in October and November, 1917, that the service battalions are
best remembered. The 6th (Service) Battalion of the Loyals was
committed to that other ill-fated campaign in Gallipoli, and later
as part of the unfortunate army which redeemed the surrender at

Kut in Mesopotamia. For the 6th Loyal North Lancashires the war was particularly harsh.

The Regiment served on every front, except Italy and West Africa. Thirteen battalions were involved at various times in France and Flanders (mostly exclusively so), one was in East Africa and Palestine, one in Gallipoli, Egypt and Mesopotamia and another in Mesopotamia and Palestine. The Second Battalion received the unique battle honour, 'Kilimanjaro', and so, with 'The Defence of Kimberley' already to their credit, the Loyals had the rare distinction of being able to claim more than one unique battle honour. But if comparisons are odious, the deeds speak for themselves.

The first and second battalions of every regiment were part of the old Regular Army, the best trained but among the smallest in Europe. Britain's reliance upon her naval might could not save her from the military strategy of Germany's Schlieffen Plan, on which the Kaiser based his initial offensive into France and the Low Countries. Our Army, which had since Waterloo been concerned primarily as a force to hold India and the Empire, was hopelessly outnumbered, outgunned and nearly defeated at the First Battle of Ypres in the late autumn and early winter of 1914.

The 1st Loyals – the title, The Loyal Regiment (North Lancashire), did not supersede The Loyal North Lancashire Regiment until 1921 – went immediately to France with Gen French's BEF. In Aldershot they had been inspected by King George V who told them:

'I have implicit confidence in you, my soldiers. Duty is your watchword and I know that your duty will be nobly done . . . Your welfare will never be absent from my thoughts . . .'

In the 2nd Brigade of the First Division, with the 2nd KRRC, the 1st Royal Sussex and the 1st Northamptons, they helped to steady the line during the depressing retreat from Mons to the Marne and back, via the Aisne, to Ypres. Here, after its heroic struggle, the Regular Army was at last reinforced and the Loyal North Lancashires' sector of the line was largely held by reservists, those time-served men, mostly approaching, or well into, middle age.

At Ypres the 1st Loyal North Lancashires dug in, largely due to the superiority of the German artillery. As Capt Hyndson of the Regiment wrote in his book, *From Mons to the First Battle of Ypres*, which was based on his diary of that campaign, 'Here we set to work to construct trenches, not so much from the point of view of defence, but with the idea of obtaining shelter from artillery fire, which is getting rather too close to be pleasant'. And so, after the failure of Sir John French's Race to the Sea, in which the BEF tried vainly to save Antwerp and to turn the Germans' northern flank, there began the trench warfare and stagnant battle of attrition which lasted throughout most of the war in France. The front line became locked even before the Second Battle of Ypres in the spring of 1915, whilst more men and a vast improvement in weapon technique, particularly that of small arms and heavy machine guns, stultified the war.

Shortage of space regrettably allows only a few words about First Ypres and the pre-eminent part played by the 1st Loyal North Lancashire Regiment. The vital six days were from 27 October to 1 November, particularly 31 October, which French described as the most critical period of his command. The Battalion held a line from the Menin Road to a point west of the village of Reutel. The German artillery was fiendish, but whilst their infantry massed opposite the 2nd KRRC and the 1st Loyal North Lancashires the Battalion was able to regroup, and at 9 am on the 31st, together with a battalion of The Gordon Highlanders, they received fresh orders to attack. On this rare occasion the two battalions advanced on the torn village of Gheluvelt with the bayonet and scattered the surprised enemy who lost heavily. Advancing again, the Loyals were on the threshold of that vital village when, shortly before noon, the enemy counter-attacked and, with the retirement of other battalions, the exhausted Loyals fell back on Hooge. But Gheluvelt was saved, in a famous action, by the gallantry of the 2nd Worcesters which brought relief to those remnants of The South Wales Borderers who had manfully held their positions in the grounds of the château. There followed the desperate and indecisive struggle for Givenchy, the British constantly suffering from inadequate artillery ammunition. During the terrible days from 27 October to 1 November the Battalion lost eight officers and over 400 other ranks, most of whom were later discovered to have been killed. So the old Regular Army perished at First Ypres.

I shall return to the 1st Battalion, soon to be completely reconstituted as a result of its terrible losses, in due course. But meanwhile the 2nd Loyal North Lancashire Regiment, as yet unchanged by the trauma which their comrades had suffered, arrived off Tanga from India on 2 November, 1914, with what was called Expeditionary Force B to take part in the operations in German East Africa. Since 1890 the old sultanate of Zanzibar had been divided by treaty between Britain and Germany, and immediately it became a second front. Here the Regiment won its second unique battle honour, 'Kilimanjaro', of which it is especially proud. But it must be recorded that the German army in East Africa, under an exceptionally fine commander in Gen Paul von Lettow-Vorbeck, managed remarkably well, considering that they had been blockaded by the Royal Navy since the outbreak of war.

The amphibious operation on Tanga, one of the chief ports of German East Africa, began on 3–4 November, 1914. The Loyals (the only British regiment in an otherwise Indian Army expedition), with the 61st Pioneers and 13th Rajputs, held the right flank of the 27th Brigade, which itself constituted the left flank of the beachhead. Artillery support, which in any case was minimal, was unable to be of much assistance owing to the thick mangrove-covered ridge above the beach; and for this reason the naval bombardment was severely reduced.

Von Lettow-Vorbeck had only four battalions of Askaris and the German Beaumstark's Battalion – one Askari battalion in the town of Tanga itself and three to the north of his headquarters, which was just south of Tanga. The German troops were half a mile to the south-east, covering the important railway workshops. But what the enemy lacked in manpower they made up in military intelligence. Indeed, from the first, Vorbeck had anticipated the raid and observation had confirmed the presence of the allied fleet.

The Loyal North Lancashires and their colleague Indian units were initially impeded by the thick, steamy rubber plantations; but covering a front of two hundred yards the battalion began to advance at noon on 4 November. Communication was from front to rear, using the telegraph line from Tanga to Signal Tower on Ras Kasone Point, just north of their landing. Lateral communication was difficult and runners had to be used. Once clear of the coastal vegetation, the North Lancashires came under heavy fire from Beaumstark's Battalion, and in the relatively open savannah country the allies forced a crossing of the railway cutting to the east of Tanga. The enemy made every use of the railway workshops from which they concentrated fire into the British and Indians as they poured across the exposed lip of the cutting. But aided by their few but well deployed Maxims the North Lancashires pressed on with the greatest heroism and, with The Kashmir Rifles, forced an entry into Tanga which was held despite severe hand-to-hand and house-to-house fighting. They captured the Kaiser Hotel and an officer climbed up and replaced the German flag with the Union Jack. The North Lancashires now held the central square and were about to consolidate when Vorbeck decided to counter-attack. Attempting to sweep around behind the battalion and the Kashmiris, he threw Beaumstark's Battalion and the 13th Company of Askaris against the flank of the Indian 101st Grenadiers. It was a master-stroke which changed the whole complexion of the battle. Fearing encirclement the brave Loyal North Lancashires and the Indians had to withdraw east of the cutting where, now with only one Maxim, they received harsh treatment; but the remaining gun provided brave and sustained covering fire whilst the lips were cleared.

Now a fateful misunderstanding occurred. Unbeknown to the allies the enemy were spent in their efforts, and were considering retirement again when they noticed the continued withdrawal of the Expeditionary Force for whom the absence of water had become a severe threat. But the whole expedition withdrew in perfect order, the crippled Indian units first, on 6 November and sailed for Kalindini in British East Africa (now Kenya).

The Loyal North Lancashires covered their withdrawal in a manner reminiscent of Corunna. Vorbeck's intelligence had kept him so well informed that he knew precisely the identity and strength of his enemy. It was therefore with complete certainty that he could write in his diary, 'the brave Loyal North Lancashires . . . set an example, in spite of heavy losses'. Chivalry still existed in war.

Vorbeck was not the only man to congratulate the Battalion. On its entry into Nairobi the Governor of British East Africa told the men:

> I am informed that you have conducted yourselves on a recent occasion with consummate bravery and exemplary discipline, under most trying conditions, and that you set an example of steadiness and pluck . . . In short, you have most worthily sustained the best traditions of your Regiment and the prestige of the British Army . . . It is quite apparent to me that you were placed at a disadvantage only on account of conditions which could not have been foreseen, and that you only need a further opportunity to add to the credit which you have already earned.

Major-Gen Aitken, who had commanded Expeditionary Force B, also praised the men for their courage.

A lull now followed while attention was devoted to the main theatre of operations in France where the battered BEF were clinging on to Ypres. But companies of the Second Battalion were redeployed, particularly at Longido, so that on Christmas Day, 1914, 3 Company, The Loyal North Lancashire Regiment, was the only allied unit occupying German territory anywhere in the world. Attacks and skirmishes followed across the frontier, but lack of space prevents any but the most cursory mention of the action on and around Mount Kilimanjaro.

After protracted and very unpleasant fighting near Lake Victoria and elsewhere, over vast distances, the situation in East Africa was altered by the arrival on 19 February, 1916, of Gen Smuts, the guerrilla general who had shown his supreme ability in bush and veldt warfare against the British during the Boer

War. In July he directed the recapture of Tanga. The man who had once directed operations against the Loyal North Lancashires was now leading them! Although the Regiment was to lose considerably more men through tropical disease than enemy action, they were to help take the offensive into the heart of German East Africa and clear the foothills of Kilimanjaro, with its coffee and tea plantations which were so vital to the German economy. This campaign, rather than any single battle, was a great distinction in the Regiment's history, and 'Kilimanjaro' represented a collective battle honour for a long and tedious war for the 2nd Loyals.

Nevertheless, Vorbeck had reached Abercorn in the far north of what is now Zambia by November, 1918; but with so much room for manoeuvre there is no doubt that this very able soldier would have eluded defeat for considerably longer had the Armistice not imposed it on him.

We must now turn to the erratic fortunes of the 6th Battalion, the Regiment's senior Service Battalion which consisted, like all so-called 'service battalions', of those brave and patriotic men who had answered Kitchener's call in 1914. Initially, 100,000 men were needed, in addition to the severely reduced strength of the Regular Army, and the Territorials whom Kitchener seemed at first anxious to keep in a purely defensive capacity. The answer to Kitchener's call for an all volunteer army was staggering, and many eager new recruits found themselves billeted in such unlikely places as railway stations, initially without rifles or uniforms. Whilst most of Kitchener's men had their first taste of action at Loos in September, 1915, or, to a greater extent, on the Somme the following July, a sizeable number were among those who reinforced the expedition to Gallipoli between 4 and 10 August, 1915. Amongst these were the 6th Loyal North Lancashires who had a very uncomfortable war against cholera, typhoid and 'Johnny' Turk.

Several members of the Cabinet and a few service chiefs had, for some time, advocated a distraction from the Western Front, although there were some generals, notably Haig, who claimed that this was where the war would be won or lost. Gallipoli was the idea solely of the First Lord of the Admiralty, Winston Churchill, but to blame him for the disaster would be unwarranted. Failure was due, in large part, to the lack of agreement among service chiefs and to the apathy of several members of the Cabinet.

The idea was for a large force (which was chiefly Anglo-Australasian) to land on the tip of the Gallipoli peninsula and assist the Navy to force the Dardanelles. Forts guarding the approaches to Constantinople would be seized and a route to provide aid to Russia would be opened. Unfortunately, there was never proper liaison between naval and military chiefs, whilst the Turks had intelligence of the landing at least six weeks before it occurred, and brought a strong defence down to meet Gen Sir Ian Hamilton's assault on 25 April, 1915. The Turks were led by the able Mustapha Kemal, under the direction of the German, Field-Marshal Liman von Sanders. No one, least of all Churchill, imagined that owing to these factors, and the inclement weather, another chapter in trench warfare would begin. It was a disastrous and humiliating campaign which, with the initial failure of the assault on the Somme, was a major disillusionment of the War. However, Britain was, on more than one occasion, within an ace of victory.

Following the landing in April, the 10th, 11th and 13th Divisions were ordered to prepare for a new amphibious operation. The *Braemar Castle* transported the thirty-one officers and 946 other ranks of the Loyals out to Gallipoli, leaving Avonmouth on 17 July. The new reinforcements pushed Gen Hamilton's army up to 110,000 men. The Navy had ceased to be of much use; already it had become a soldiers' war. On 31 July the 13th Division was sent temporarily to Mudros on Lemnos Island in the Aegean where the 6th Loyals' first casualties were sustained. From here, in an attempt to reinforce the sadly depleted Australians and New Zealanders at Anzac Cove, the Division was moved to nearby Suvla Bay.

The 13th replaced the worn out 29th Division, which was soon to reappear on the Somme, and the newcomers moved to Anzac on 4 August where they joined Australian, New Zealand and Indian troops. Here they were to attempt to gain the Heights of Koja Chemen Tepe and the northern seaward ridges as part of the grand overall strategy to lure the Turks from various inland hideouts. At all events, the allies had to push inland and sever Turkish strongholds in the central highlands. The 13th Division (less five battalions) was ordered to join the Australians and New Zealanders from Anzac Cove in a frontal attack on Chunuk Bair Ridge. The 38th Brigade was held in reserve, but the 6th Loyal North Lancashire was detached as a reinforcement for the New Zealand Brigade for the Chunuk Bair fighting to control the Narrows below.

The 6th Loyals were called up with the 5th Wiltshire and the 10th Hampshire in support. The Wiltshires were almost annihilated, and the 6th Loyals fared little better. Gen Hamilton's despatch was graphic:

> Generals fought in the ranks and men dropped their scientific weapons and caught one another by the throat. So desperate a fight cannot be described. The Turks came on again and again, fighting magnificently, calling upon the name of God. Our men stood to it and maintained, by many a deed of daring, the old traditions of their race. There was no flinching. They died in the ranks where they stood.

The casualties were astronomical, and the 38th Brigade Commander lay dead with his men on the crest of the ridge. But the Turks had held out. Reinforcements arrived, but it was too late. During November torrential rain hampered progress, followed by blast ice.

Thereafter thoughts turned in Whitehall to evacuation. At Suvla were the 13th and three more divisions, and from 10th December the withdrawal began to proceed by skilful degrees, so that by the 20th the 6th Loyals embarked on the *Ascanius* and sailed for Alexandria. But they were not there long. Now another campaign needed swift attention, and under the command of Gen Maude the Battalion faced the unpleasant war in Mesopotamia to save the disaster which had been incurred at Kut simultaneously with that in Gallipoli.

There was something almost biblical about the situation in the
Middle East in 1914. Nothing had changed for centuries. The
Turks had held Jerusalem since before the Crusades, whilst
further east, in Mesopotamia, they amassed the largest empire
to which the Iraquis had been subject since the Romans, or even
since the conquests of Alexander the Great. This country, the
supposed Garden of Eden, had witnessed the Fall of Man and
the death of Abel at the hand of his brother, Cain. From Genesis'
record of the first human slaughter there had been no peace in
the land. But Lawrence would restore the Hejaz of Arabia to
the Arabs and Jerusalem would, in part, be returned to Christen-
dom, whilst, after terrible losses, the British and Indian forces
would eventually smash the eastern approaches of the old Otto-
man Empire.

The campaigns in Mesopotamia, notably the first, were ill-
planned, disease-ridden and fought by the forgotten armies of
the First World War. India, of course, was the reason for
Britain's involvement in the area, but Britain's influence over
the sub-continent was irreparably damaged by the surrender of
her garrison at Kut-al-Amara. The British misfortune begun at
Kut in 1915–16 was completed at Singapore in 1942 – they were
the second largest and the largest surrenders respectively in
British military history. Even courage was hardly apparent in
what Doughty had called 'days deadly drowned in the sun of the
summer wilderness'. But among the squalor of that dusty and
diseased battleground the North Lancashires had particular cause
for pride and none for shame.

Major-Gen Sir Charles Townshend, who had commanded the
first British Expeditionary Force to Mesopotamia in 1915, made
the same elementary mistake on the Tigris that Burgoyne had
made on the Hudson, but with even more disastrous results.
Rather than advance on a broad front from the south-east, the
British and Indian force was tempted by lack of numbers to sever
the Turks by attempting to hold the right bank of the Tigris
upstream from Basra. As on the Hudson the initial advance was
rapid, but lines of supply were becoming daily more attenuated
in hostile country. Townshend reached a point eighty miles

beyond Kut, but was eventually beaten by the Turks at Ctesi-phon, only twenty miles from Baghdad. The allies now fell back on Kut where they were besieged for 143 days, from 5 December, until, on 29 April, 1916, Townshend surrendered the survivors of a garrison of 5,746 men. (Even this figure is nearly 2,000 fewer than The Loyal North Lancashire Regiment lost fatally through-out the War.) The world was stunned. Again the British Empire had shown that it was not invincible – even on India's very door-step.

The situation had to be redeemed, and another force under Major-Gen Sir Stanley Maude retook Kut in February, 1917, and advanced beyond Baghdad. This was Britain's first major success in the Middle East. Among the 30,000 infantry and 127 guns under command of Gen Gorringe's Tigris Corps was the 13th Division (hoping for better fortune on this errand of mercy than it had found in Gallipoli), consisting, as before, of the 38th, 39th and 40th Brigades and divisional artillery. The 38th Brigade, of course, consisted entirely of Lancastrians, including the 6th Loyals. The 13th Division successfully launched the initial assault.

As the force proceeded northward from below Kut by slow and painful degrees against an intrepid foe, news of the 6th Loyals, as of other brave battalions, came back to encourage Maude and Gorringe. The Loyals earned undying praise from the Allied Headquarters and field commanders, and one must mention a few of the despatches.

With a strength of twenty-two officers and 949 other ranks the 6th Loyal North Lancashire began their first assault from Sheikh Saad about forty miles downstream from Kut, at 4.55 am on 5 April, 1916. This and the second assault were carried successfully. By 7 am the Division had captured the enemy's fourth and fifth lines of trenches. This was a triumphant day for the men of the Red Rose. The official history of the Mesopo-tamian campaign, *The Mesopotamian Campaign*, Vol II, records that evening's achievements baldly:

About 7 pm the 38th and 39th Brigades, which, passing through the 40th, were to deliver the assault, began forming up in four lines, and at about 7.15 the artillery bombardment commenced. The four lines of the 38th Brigade consisted each of one battalion on a frontage of one thousand yards, the 6th Loyal North Lancashire being in front, with the 6th King's Own, 6th East Lancashire and the 6th South Lancashire behind them in that order . . . At 7.35 the 38th and 39th Brigades began their advance; and in spite of strong resistance by the enemy, the 38th Brigade had, by a fine advance, captured their objective by 8.15 pm . . .

There now followed the expensive assault on the Sannaiyat position, about twenty miles downstream from Kut. On that day, 9 April, 1916, the fighting was so fierce that four Victoria Crosses were awarded, one of them going to the Rev W. F. R. Addison, the Church of England chaplain attached to the 6th Loyals. All day he had comforted the dying and wounded in open country, completely regardless of his own safety. The 13th Division as a whole had sustained 1,807 casualties and the 6th Loyals was reduced by over 26 per cent of its strength.

The Battalion was constantly in demand, and on one occasion, in the operation against the Dahra Bend of the Tigris in February, 1917, it was attached to the 40th Brigade to capture the objective. This is evidence of the great reputation it had won. But, as the despatch says, 'early on the 15th the Loyal North Lancashires captured a strong point opposite our left, which enfiladed the approaches to the enemy's right and centre, the retiring Turks losing heavily from our machine gun fire.' Through heavy rain the allies completed the recapture of Kut, whilst Maude pressed home his advance on the right towards Baghdad.

But perhaps the Battalion's most memorable feat in Mesopotamia was the crossing of the Diyala River by a large portion of one company on the southern approaches to Baghdad. Soon after midnight on 9 March the Loyal North Lancashires launched their pontoons just above a point where another battalion had come to grief the previous night. By the time a hundred men of the company were established on the north bank the Turks woke up to the danger of the operation and put up an intense defence. Pontoons were sunk, ferrying ceased and the small bridgehead was cut off except for minimal help from the river where desperate attempts were still being made to get lines across to facilitate the transport of ammunition. But countless men died in the water during these vain attempts. Somehow the bridgehead hung on while it was depleted in men and ammunition. Reinforcements and attachments from other regiments had come forward, so that in little over two days the 6th North Lancashires had lost over a thousand men and practically all its officers. But the bridgehead miraculously held out. In *The Mesopotamian Campaign*, Vol III, we read that 'The Turkish account of their attempts to drive out this British detachment affords a fine testimony to the gallant tenacity of these men of Lancashire . . .', whilst *The Life of General Maude* records that 'Some men of the Loyal North Lancashire did manage to gain a footing but they maintained a grip upon a small loop in the river embankment, unsupported except for fire from the other side, for twenty-four hours, in spite of every effort of the enemy to dislodge them'. From Gen Maude himself, soon to die of typhoid, came the sincere message.

Please convey my best congratulations to my old Division and especially to the die-hards of the Loyal North Lancs. who stuck to their post so grimly and manfully.

Today, at this point, there stands a fine bridge (replacing a temporary structure known as 'Lancashire Bridge'), and upon it is a plaque which reads,

To the Glorious Memory of the Heroic Dead who are buried near this spot and who gave their lives to carry out a brilliant feat of arms in the crossing of the Diyala River on 10 March, 1917 in the face of a strongly entrenched enemy. Pro Patria.

We must now return to that theatre of war where we briefly began – France and Flanders. The Regiment was represented by one or frequently several battalions at all the great engagements in France. From the point at which we left it after First Ypres the 1st Battalion was at Neuve Chapelle, Loos, on the Somme, at Arras, Vimy Ridge, Passchendaele, at the Battle of the Lys during the German Spring Offensive in 1918, at Béthune, St

Quentin and the Sambre Canal. The 2nd, after its campaign in East Africa, was in Egypt and Palestine and the final battles in France. The 3rd was a draft finding unit. The 1/4th was at Festubert, Arras, on the Somme and at Third Ypres. The 2/4th was at Passchendaele, the Scarpe and Cambrai; the 3/4th was a reserve battalion. The 1/5th was at Armentières, Second and Third Ypres, the Somme, the Hindenburg Line and Arras; the 2/5th at Ploegsteert Wood, Armentières, Poelcappelle, Arras and Cambrai; the 3/5th was a reserve battalion and the 4/5th was at Armentières and Passchendaele. We have already traced the record of the 6th. The 7th was at Loos, Neuve Chapelle, on the Somme and its many battles from Albert to Pozières, along the central axis from Albert to Bapaume, and at Third Ypres and Messines. The 8th was on the Somme and at Ploegsteert Wood. The 9th was also on the Somme, at Ploegsteert Wood, Messines, Pilckem, Béthune and the Lys. The 10th, yet another Somme battalion, was in the Loos Salient, at Arras, the Scarpe and Third Ypres. The 11th was in reserve, whilst a territorial battalion, the 1/12th, was at Vimy, on the Somme and the Ancre, at Salonika, in Macedonia, Egypt and Palestine. The 2/12th, the 13th and 14th were in reserve; and lastly the 15th was at Poperinghe and the final Battle of Ypres. This exhaustive list mentions only the Regiment's major actions, but it may be seen that at various stages it was engaged in every important and protracted battle or campaign, and that not a name in that list of infamy is absent. To select particular occasions, where overall the Regiment sustained the deaths of 357 officers and 7,232 other ranks in all theatres and won sixty-eight battle honours, is an invidious but necessary task.

It will be noticed at once that a substantial proportion of the Regiment fought on the Somme, although only the 7th Battalion seemed likely to be concerned on that terrible opening day, 1 July, 1916. But at least on that occasion they were fortunate. All day the 19th (Western) Division had remained in reserve on the Tara-Usna Line outside Albert. The Division was to have followed the initial assault of 7.30 am which had come to such grief before the German machine guns, basically undamaged by the week-long

British artillery bombardment. That the Division should follow up the anticipated success of this assault with the cavalry to Bapaume was therefore out of the question. Instead, they were to attack at 5 pm and the four Lancashire battalions of the 19th Division, including the 7th Loyals, waited anxiously for an assignment that was supposed to succeed, where a whole division had failed earlier that day. However, only in the extreme south of the Somme sector, opposite Mametz and Montauban, had any success been gained, and further assaults on 1 July were eventually considered to be too dangerous. So, at the last minute, with a sense of relief from men who had watched an anticipated military triumph turn into a bloodbath, these particular Lancastrians were marched back to the rear. According to Pte C. B. Mawbey of the 7th Loyal North Lancashires,

> The attack was cancelled only minutes before it was due to start and we went out to some high ground behind Albert where we had refreshment and, illustrating the incongruities of war, were addressed by a visiting bishop and entertained by the divisional band.

But the 7th North Lancashires' turn would come in due course.

They were duly in action in the area of La Boiselle, which they eventually captured with the 19th Division on 5 September. It was here that Lt T. O. L. Wilkinson won the Victoria Cross. His citation reads,

> For most conspicuous bravery. During an attack, when a party of another unit were returning without their machine gun, Lieut Wilkinson rushed forward and with two of his men, got the gun into action, and held up the enemy until they were relieved.
>
> Later, when the advance was checked during a bombing attack, he forced his way forward and found four or five men of different units stopped by a solid block of earth, over which the enemy were throwing bombs.
>
> With great pluck and promptness he mounted a machine gun on the top of the parapet and dispersed the enemy bombers. Subsequently he made two most gallant attempts to bring in a wounded man, but in the second attempt he was shot through the heart, just before reaching the man.

Throughout the day he set a magnificent example of courage and self-sacrifice.

The 7th Loyals remained during the Somme offensive in the centre of the British line until November, but their initial brief taste of action there finished on 7 September when their trenches were temporarily taken over by the 13th Battalion, The Rifle Brigade.

Neighbours in the 7th Brigade were the 8th Service Battalion which sustained heavy losses, but which were present at the capture of the heavily defended town of Orvilliers which, like La Boiselle, had eluded Gen Rawlinson's offensive on 1 July. Among those of the 8th Battalion who had been killed only a few days earlier was Lt R. B. B. Jones who also won a posthumous Victoria Cross, as his citation relates,

> . . . for most conspicuous bravery. He was holding, with his platoon, a crater recently captured from the enemy. About 7.30 pm the enemy exploded a mine forty yards to his right, and at the same time put a heavy barrage of fire on our trenches, thus isolating the platoon.
>
> They then attacked in overwhelming numbers. Lt Jones kept his men together, steadying them by his fine example, and shot no less than fifteen of the enemy as they advanced, counting them aloud as he did so to cheer his men. When his ammunition was expended he took a bomb, but was shot through the head while getting up to throw it.
>
> His splendid courage had so encouraged his men that when they had no more ammunition, or bombs, they threw stones and ammunition boxes at the enemy till only nine of the platoon were left. Finally they were compelled to retire.

This, with the VC won by Pte H. Kenny for 'most conspicuous bravery' in bringing in, on six occasions, wounded men under fire, the notice of which appeared in *The London Gazette* on 30 March, 1916, brought to four the Victoria Crosses won by men with or attached to The Loyal North Lancashire Regiment during the War.

Also in the 25th Division was the 9th Battalion, another Service Battalion of the kind which seemed to constitute such a large proportion of Rawlinson's Fourth Army and which had little or no more military experience than to be slaughtered on the Somme. But, like so many other regiments, the North Lancashires seemed to produce men from nowhere as they struggled forward, yard by yard, to capture those objectives which Haig had hoped would fall on 1 July, and so allow his cavalry to sweep on towards the frontier. All the many battalions of the Regiment on the Somme sector were in the centre between Albert and Bapaume where the worst carnage had initially been wrought.

Another glance at the list of names will show how frequently that of Loos appears. Apart from Second Ypres it was the bloodiest battle of 1915 on the Western Front where gas was used by both sides. Loos was intended to be an Anglo-French action. A British force of two divisions in Haig's 1st Army Corps – Haig did not succeed Field-Marshal French until the end of 1915 – attacked the line, Loos–Hulluch–Haisnes, in the hope of dislodging the Germans and securing the northern approaches to Lens which was threatened in the south by the French at Souchez. Throughout the last week of September the battle raged as the opposing armies captured and recaptured ground which added to British military history the nightmare names of 'Hill 70' and the Hohenzollern Redoubt. In the end the British captured Loos and their line advanced 4,000 yards over a 7,000-yard front. As for the 1st Loyal North Lancashires the casualties on 25 September alone reached the appalling figure of sixteen officers and 489 other ranks.

Passchendaele, known more formally as the Third Battle of Ypres, had particular association with the Loyal North Lancashires and deserves particular mention. The victor here was the weather, helped by merciless shelling which turned the ridge into a quagmire where frequently those men who slipped off the duckboards drowned in the mud. Third Ypres persisted from the end of July until early November, 1917. Haig, now Commander-in-Chief of the BEF, hoped to launch a strong attack in the summer which would turn the German right and regain the French coast. A successful advance from the Ypres Salient towards Bruges might achieve this object, besides ensuring the safety of Ypres, and a necessary part of the operation was the capture of Passchendaele Ridge which, with Messines and Vimy Ridges already captured, would give the British a commanding position over Flanders.

Here the territorial battalions of the Loyal North Lancashires were heavily committed. None fared worse or conducted itself with greater courage than the 2/5th. The Battalion's War Diary for 24 October reads:

> ... the leading waves had scarcely gone more than fifty yards before they came under an intense machine gun barrage which caused a great number of casualties, and it seemed that our barrage had missed locating the positions of the enemy machine guns. All the company officers of the Battalion became casualties during the early stages of the attack and the sergeants and junior non-commissioned officers then carried on the advance in a most determined manner. Small groups of men reached and held some shell-craters about 500 yards in advance of our original line; and it was only by reason of the particularly heavy losses and the very thin line that was being held that it was decided to withdraw to our original position and there consolidate.

> The enemy seemed to have anticipated the attack and had pushed forward small groups of men very close to our line under cover of the darkness. These groups were untouched by our barrage and surprised the leading waves, thus causing the heavy casualties in the initial stages of the attack. The enemy's snipers were especially efficient.

> The ground which had to be advanced over was dreadful, and it speaks well for the men that they got along at all as it was mostly impassable. The German machine guns were mostly employed in shell-holes, bringing a cross-fire to bear on the Battalion frontage; though covers were used for the rifles it was found almost impossible to fire them owing to the mud which collected on the rifles as the men fell in and out of shell-holes waist deep in water.

Owing to the heavy casualties among the officers Passchendaele became, like Inkerman, a soldiers' battle. But the Battalion hung on, and it fell to those who relieved it to be among the final victors of this singularly unpleasant battle. In two days the 2/5th had suffered 288 casualties.

To the 2/5th also goes the credit for the fall of Cambrai on 10 October, 1918, and there is no doubt that they were among the first

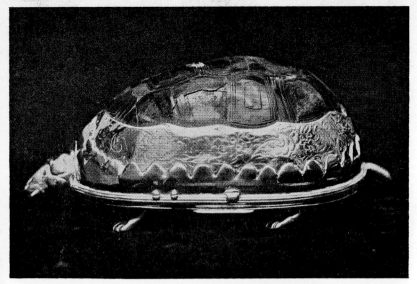

7. *The Maida Tortoise: a valuable relic of the Battle of Maida*

8. *The 47th raiding a stockade in Burma in 1826*

9. *Major R. T. Farren, a hero of the Crimean War*

10. *Pte J. McDermond trying to save the life of Lt-Col Haly during the Battle of Inkerman on 5 November, 1856. He was subsequently awarded the Victoria Cross for his gallantry*

British troops to enter the town where they found a large clothing store which contained what was discovered to be the uniform
which the Germans were to have worn on their triumphal entry
into Paris. Great sport was had by the 2/5th Loyal North Lancashires, and probably no troops in the British Army returned
home with a more fascinating collection of booty.

One campaign remains briefly to be mentioned – Palestine and
the capture of Jerusalem. The 1/12th had taken part in the
malaria-ridden but successful war in Macedonia, but was moved
next to Palestine where the British campaign had been impeded
by unimaginative and unskilful generalship, which was largely
responsible for heavy losses when, in April, 1917, Gen Allenby
was appointed to the Middle Eastern Command. After the British
had suffered two defeats earlier in the year, at Magrunstein and
the First Battle of Gaza, Allenby was given express orders that
Jerusalem was to be captured by Christmas. Allenby, who had
been a sharp critic of the Somme offensive, could now abandon
on his own initiative the folly of frontal infantry assault, which
the Turks had so welcomed, and employ his tactics of feints and
deception.
Even against Field-Marshal von Falkanhayn, whom the Turks
had imported from France to command them, he was to prove
the master of Palestine.
The offensive for the capture of Jerusalem began with the
Third Battle of Gaza, sometimes known as the Battle of Beer-
sheba, on 31 October, 1917, in which the various companies of the
Loyal North Lancashires found themselves split up among
different brigades, and detailed for the vital – if uncomfortable –
task of road building for the transport of Allenby's precious water
supplies and the movement of troops in mountainous areas. For
the latter purpose, also, patrols of the Battalion crept devasta-
tingly upon unsuspecting picquets guarding Turkish wells, since
shortage of water was Allenby's chief concern.
The Loyals had been in the 60th Division and their Corps
Commander, Lt-Gen Sir Philip Chetwode – later Field-Marshal
Lord Chetwode, Commander-in-Chief, India – wrote after the

capture of Jerusalem to Major-Gen Shea, the divisional commander,

My dear Shea,
   Will you please thank your troops for the spendid work they have put in on the laborious and uncongenial task of road-making in your area, which has not only rendered possible further offensive operations, but in the event of the enemy ever being in the position to attack Jerusalem has quadrupled our powers of defence by permitting the free movement of troops in the mountains.

Whilst the North Lancashires should, on the one hand, have had to suffer this mundane work, on the other some of them were gloriously rewarded, and it was to two sergeants of the 1/12th The Loyal North Lancashire Regiment that the Turkish commander surrendered Jerusalem on 8 December, 1917, after 1,280 years of Islamic rule. The following day Gen Allenby made his famous entry into the old City on foot, impressing everyone with the humility of a true victor, leading his white charger by its reins.

We have now covered, if regrettably inadequately, every theatre of war in which The Loyal North Lancashire Regiment served. One can only hope that we have had an insight into the spirit that saw them through the terrible battles and the grim tedium of the First World War, remembering at the same time that other dimension of war which inspired Wilfred Owen, himself killed only a week before the Armistice, to write of a colleague in a Lancashire regiment (the Manchesters),

'I have perceived much beauty
   In the hoarse oaths that kept our courage straight;
   Heard music in the silentness of duty;
   Found peace where shell storms spouted reddest spate.'

The Loyal North Lancashire Regiment had kept their courage straight.

CHAPTER 12

Years of Relative Peace, 1919–1939

THE duties which the Loyals had to fulfil after the War were in complete contrast to the rather unimaginative campaigns of attrition to which they had become accustomed. Now the Army was used very evidently as a means of supporting diplomatic and commercial manœuvres in nearly every part of the world. Whilst the strength of the Army may have dwindled alarmingly between the Wars, there was as much scope as ever for the soldier who enlisted because he wanted to see the world. On both officers and men alike considerable diplomatic responsibility had devolved.

Ireland soon claimed the attention of many regiments (as, regrettably, it had done during the War), and both battalions of The Loyal Regiment (as it had become known in 1921) were engaged in that year, the First Battalion having been recalled from Malta where it was then stationed. 'The troubles', as they were rather euphemistically called, were particularly near home for The Loyal Regiment which, coming from Lancashire, inevitably had several Irishmen in it.

No sooner were the Loyals withdrawn from Ireland than the First Battalion found itself involved in the notorious incident at Chanak on the Dardanelles. Here they were the sole garrison when the trouble broke out (when one remembers Lahore and Kimberley it would seem that the Regiment had an uncomfortable habit of being the only British troops stationed where trouble occurred). The Battalion shared for six months in 1922 the duties of holding the perimeter posts of areas disputed by the Turks at Chanak.

The Battalion's next posting could not have been more remote from everything previously experienced, for the following year they were responsible for keeping open railway communication between Peking and the Yellow Sea, in accordance with treaty agreement. The 1st Loyals now spent twelve months on the North-West Frontier of India, whilst, in 1937, it was the turn of the Second Battalion to police an area of China by undergoing similar duties in Shanghai where Britain also had commercial interests, secured by treaty. At this time, however, fighting was taking place between China and Japan, in the vicinity of the city, and the situation did not augur well. For six months the Battalion had to help secure the British sector of the international defence line in order to safeguard the lives and property of British residents and merchants. It was the 2nd Loyals, together with the several other British battalions in this part of the world just before the war, who were sent to form the nucleus of the army which was to be given the hopeless task of defending Malaya and Singapore.

A year before the despatch of the Second Battalion to Shanghai the First Loyals were sent to Palestine and within a few weeks were on active service. The pogrom of the Jews in Germany by Hitler led to a huge influx of refugees into Palestine. This caused the greatest resentment among the Arab population who organized a general strike on 18 April, 1936, which quickly developed into armed rebellion. At that time there were only two infantry battalions in the country, the Loyals in the north, based on Haifa, and the Camerons in the south, based on Jerusalem. Operating in company and platoon detachments, the Loyals were continuously engaged for the next five months defending the unarmed Jewish settlements, carrying out cordon and search operations against Arab villages from which the rebels were operating, patrolling and guarding the railways, escorting road convoys and carrying out sweep operations in the hills around Jenin and Nazareth. Minor engagements were frequent and the Battalion achieved many notable successes.

In February the Battalion had been joined by Major G. W. R. Templer who later became one of this country's most distinguished soldiers. Like Kekewich, he had been posted to the Loyals from The Inniskillings on being made a brevet major, and was later to return to his old Regiment, briefly as a captain and then as a brevet lieutenant-colonel. For his outstanding work as a Company Commander he was awarded the DSO. Altogether the Battalion received two DSOs, three MCs, five DCMs and four MMs for its work in northern Palestine. Before it left for England in the spring of 1937 the Governor paid a special visit to Haifa to thank and congratulate the Battalion.

The Loyals have always had a fine sporting record, and it is appropriate that their last Colonel, Brig G. A. Rimbault, should have become Director of the Army Sport Control Board after his retirement. The Regiment has shown a catholic ability, ranging from hunting and polo to cricket, football, hockey, athletics and swimming, winning the Army Swimming Championship in 1969. Particularly remembered between the wars is Lt J. R. Cole, an outstanding rugby player who represented the Army, the Combined Services, the Harlequins and the Barbarians, and won three England Trial Caps. But the particular sport in which the Loyals excelled has always been boxing. The 1st Battalion won the King's Shield in 1914 and the 2nd Battalion won it no less than five times between 1924 and 1936, while individual Army champions are too many to list here. Probably the most famous name in the boxing annals of the Regiment is that of Sgt 'Dusty' Miller, unbeaten in his era and subsequently the trainer and mentor of innumerable Loyals, Sandhurst and Army teams.

Remaining in abeyance until 1920, the Territorial Battalions of the Loyals were under the colonelcy of the man who has been called 'the King of Lancashire', the 17th Earl of Derby, KG, GCB, GCVO – of the 4th Battalion since 1909 and the 5th since 1899. This represents a remarkable record of longevity, particularly since he still took a keen interest in the Regiment's progress throughout the Second World War, and until his death in 1948. As with the regular battalions themselves (under the colonelcy of Gen Sir James Willcocks, GCB, GCMG, KCSI, DSO), the Great War did not disturb the colonelcy, and this stability and continuity took the Loyals into the inter-war period. The only colonelcy which was broken was that of the 3rd Loyals (in 1919 included with the regulars) when, in 1914, they suffered the death of their Colonel, the great Field-Marshal Lord Roberts, VC, who was the only man who ever held eight sets of post-nominal letters.

The advent of the Second World War disturbed the formation of many of the Regiment's territorial battalions. The 4th became the 62nd Searchlight Regiment (RA) in 1938, the 5th (of which we shall read later) became the 18th Reconnaissance Battalion in 1941 and was present at the fall of Singapore; of the 6th, 7th, 8th and 9th Battalions we shall read in the next chapter, as they distinguished themselves in North-West Europe and Burma. The 10th formed the 50th in 1940 and remained in home defence in Yorkshire until 1942 when it replaced the 2nd Loyals, lost in Singapore, and fought with much bravery in northern Italy, particularly on the trying feature known as Monte Grande. Neither the 30th nor the 31st saw service during the War. But the Loyals managed to send four battalions (two of which were converted into regiments) abroad during the War – two to North-West Europe, one to Singapore and one to Burma. In a sense, it could be argued that 'the Saturday Night Soldier', who is pre-pared to give up his spare time to become trained, possesses an element of enthusiasm which he shares to the same degree as the regular soldier. Comparisons are odious, but there is no doubt that among those many battalions which enlivened the towns and villages of northern Lancashire with their enthusiasm, the spirit fully existed to meet Hitler's challenge in 1939. Meanwhile, Preston's Home Guard unit was also affiliated to the Regiment.

As for the two regulars, they were, like their forbears in 1914, exceptionally well trained, albeit sadly undermanned, in an Empire which was a unique training ground. The Second Battalion was soon to become disarmed after its brave but hope-less struggle in the Far East, whilst the senior Battalion was ready to prove itself as one of the finest units in Lord Gort's Expeditionary Force to France.

CHAPTER 13

The Second World War: Defence of the Dunkirk Perimeter

I T has often been said that Britain loses all her battles except
the last. Whilst that might be a slight exaggeration, albeit with
a grain of truth, it may be truer to say that Britain frequently
loses the first. In no war was this better exemplified than the
Second World War when Guderian's armoured corps of the
Blitzkrieg swept the British Expeditionary Force out of France
and the Low Countries in five weeks, between 10 May and 18
June, 1940 (as it had done in Poland), the bulk of the survivors
departing, of course, from Dunkirk between 29 May and 4 June.
The swift and brilliant German strategy, which took them to
the French coast at Abbeville, cut the allies in half. Whilst the
51st Highland Division and hangers-on surrendered on French
orders at St Valéry-en-Caux, and another gallant garrison (largely
of the KRRC and the Rifle Brigade) was eventually forced to
surrender at Calais and the 20th Guards Brigade, after equally
heroic resistance, failed to hold Boulogne, it was at Dunkirk that
the miracle occurred. Calais and Boulogne may have made this
possible. At Dunkirk 338,226 British and French troops were
evacuated by an armada of craft from cruisers to rowing boats
in the greatest military legend of modern times. The Loyals,
represented in the British Expeditionary Force only by the First
Battalion, stood and held back the Germans on the line of the
Bergues–Furnes Canal at Bergues in a rearguard action reminiscent of the old 81st at Corunna.

The 1st Loyals had in Lt-Col John Sandie a Commanding
Officer with great powers of leadership which were reflected in
the fine fighting spirit of the Battalion. The Battalion had lingered
in France through the 'Phoney War', had advanced to meet the
German offensive on 10 May and, like most of the BEF, had

been driven back over the Dendre and the Escaut until they found themselves bottled up in Dunkirk, with their backs to the sea and little hope of ever reaching England. It was here that their story – more, even, than that of most battalions at Dunkirk – properly begins.

The defence of Dunkirk was organized on 27 May and it was arranged that the French should be responsible for a sector stretching westward of a line from the coast at Gravelines to the medieval fortified town of Bergues, some seven miles south-east of Dunkirk. Two days later the First Division, in which the Loyals served with the Second Brigade, commanded by Major-Gen Alexander who on the 31st was given the command of I Corps and responsibility for the evacuation, entered the perimeter and the Loyals took up a defensive position on the sandhills near the coastal resort of Bray-Dunes, east of Dunkirk. The whole operation was complicated by French and Belgian refugees, pouring in from the east, as much as by the strafing and dive-bombing of the Luftwaffe.

By now the evacuation had begun and on the evening of the 29th the Loyals proceeded in groups towards Dunkirk. Mean-while, rumours persisted of successful German infiltration from the south, particularly around Bergues and along the Bergues–Furnes Canal which marked the southern boundary of the peri-meter. In this area there were still the 139th Brigade and the 46th Division, the latter having been in France for only a month, with virtually no artillery. Otherwise, from a scratch force under Brig Usher which had been detailed to assist the French, C Company of the 2nd Royal Warwickshires had distinguished themselves by beating off an enemy assault on Bergues later on 28 May. The old fortress of Bergues, at the confluence of three canals and the junction of the British and French armies, was essential to the defence of the Dunkirk perimeter. On that day the 46th Division was concentrated behind the Canal des Moeres, the 139th Brigade being deployed in Bergues itself. But that was not enough. To the 2nd Brigade, about to embark for England, came the order to send one battalion to Bergues immediately. To quote from the Brigade's War Diary, 'the Loyals were given this task, and turning back from the sea and the ships, they marched the seven miles back to Bergues'. Capt C. G. T. Dean wrote in the Regimental History, *The Loyal Regiment (North Lancashire), 1919–1953*, vol III, that 'No more responsible, and less enviable duty could well be imagined, as the unit charged with the defence of this key point could entertain little hope of being evacuated.' Lt-Col Sandie, after a march which had been delayed by some shelling, entered Bergues by the Ypres Gate, and reported his Battalion's safe arrival to the 2nd Brigade Commander, Brig C. E. Hudson, VC, from whom, hurriedly scribbled in very adverse conditions, came the reply from Dunkirk that will always be prized by the Loyals' veterans:

> 'Well done, John, if other blokes could do the sort of thing the Loyals have done, it wouldn't be necessary to ask the Loyals to do the things they do! . . . Tell them how well I think they have done.'

Brig Usher and his staff now left for Dunkirk and Lt-Col Sandie proceeded to deploy his Battalion, together with men from the 2nd Royal Warwicks, and a composite company formed from stragglers of The Royal Artillery, The Welsh Guards, The Lincolnshire Regiment and The Royal West Kent Regiment, at various strategic points in Bergues.

Apart mainly from Artillery units, only a few Infantry battalions now remained outside Dunkirk itself. To the east of Bergues the 2/5th Sherwood Foresters took up positions on 30 May along a two-mile frontage of the canal, opposite Hoymille and Warhem. Behind them the 9th Foresters were deployed along the canal, whilst the rest of the 139th Brigade, the 2/5th Royal Leicesters (now only seventy-four all ranks) was in reserve at Nôtre Dame des Neiges, two miles north of Bergues.

That night the enemy opened a heavy bombardment, and although the Loyals held Bergues the 2/5th Foresters had to retire three miles beyond the canal to the Canal des Moeres. C Company of the Royal Warwickshires was ordered to move to the Bergues–Furnes Canal, from the bridge opposite Hoymille to cover a distance of 1,500 yards to the Pont-à-Moutons.

Next day, 31 May, the Loyals continued to hold Bergues against heavy shelling. At noon the 9th Foresters departed northward and were given a basket of wine by the PMC of the Loyals' Officers' Mess as a parting present! Later the Germans approached closer from the south.

Whilst the evacuation from Dunkirk was proceeding, the perimeter divisions (1, 46 and 50) and a brigade of the 42nd held their positions against strengthening German attacks, until at noon on 1 June Sandie ordered his men to evacuate Bergues. D Company took up positions opposite the Ypres Gate and at 12.30 pm HQ and B companies moved back to Coudekerque. At this moment it was learned that the Germans had crossed the Bergues–Furnes Canal in strength and that a platoon of the 2nd Royal Warwickshires had been overrun. But the enemy was gallantly halted by a troop of the 5th Inniskilling Dragoon Guards, the 46th Division's cavalry.

Moving south again, Lt-Col Sandie counter-attacked the enemy over the flooded ground, encouraging his men 'with more vigorous action'. At 5.30 pm the battalion was established again along the canal bank.

But now, with the Germans pushed back and the main evacuation exceeding all expectation, came the opportunity at last to withdraw northward; and it was a very weary Battalion that marched, very much under individual company commands, towards the port. D Company did not leave the Ypres Gate until 10.30 pm on 1 June, so that the Battalion's retirement was covered in the proper way. But although the Beachmaster's voice could be heard shouting, 'Loyals; this way, Loyals', fully loaded craft at the end of the mole meant that the bulk of the Battalion could not be evacuated until 7.00 pm on 2 June. Major Gibson's party did not reach Dover until 8.30 am next day, Lt-Col Sandie following his Second-in-Command half an hour later. His was probably the last battalion to return. All witnesses will testify to the heart-rending sight of the thousands of French troops, waiting in vain for their turn at the end of the East Mole at Dunkirk while their doomed comrades were still gallantly holding the shrunken perimeter.

Lt-Col Sandie received the DSO; CQMS R. Lyons, Sgt G.
Bolton and Sgt R. Sherriff the DCM; and Sgt G. Morris and
L/Cpl A. F. Gardner the MM. For the Regiment itself Dunkirk
has always had special meaning, and accordingly it deserves a
special chapter.

CHAPTER 14

The Second World War: Defeat into Victory

WHILST the 1st Loyals were now involved in home defence, in preparation for the invasion which was expected daily, the Second Battalion was caught up in that morale-sapping campaign on the other side of the world – the hopeless effort to save Malaya and Singapore. There the Loyals was one of the first British battalions on Singapore Island itself where the garrison began mobilizing on 2 September, 1939; and two days later the 2nd Loyals set about wiring and strengthening the beaches along the southern coast and the port which was mistakenly thought to be the most vulnerable sector.

Japanese hostility, particularly around the international zones in China, had steadily increased since the fall of France. In December, 1939, the Battalion had moved temporarily to Kuala Lumpur for training, and the following June British units were brought back from Tientsin and Shanghai. On 14 September the 1st and 2nd Malay Infantry Brigades were brought down to the Changi area of Singapore and the beach defences of the south-west corner. The 1st Brigade was now commanded by Brig G. R. R. Williams of the Loyals and under him were the 2nd Battalion, whose place as their Commanding Officer had been taken by Lt-Col Mordaunt Elrington, a direct descendant of both the founder of the 47th, Gen John Mordaunt, and Lt-Col Elrington of the 47th who had distinguished himself during the Pindari Wars and in Burma. Elrington now organized his sector of the south-east corner. Throughout the spring and summer of 1941 reinforcements arrived and Lt-Gen A. E. Percival, the Commander-in-Chief in Malaya, decided to protect the oil and rubber in Malacca and Johore, for which he made the Eighth Australian Division responsible (Major-Gen G. Bennett).

Hostilities broke out on 7/8 December, 1941, when the Japanese struck simultaneously at Pearl Harbor and at several points astride the Burma–Siam frontier along the east coast. On 10 December they sank the battleships *Prince of Wales* and *Repulse*, and further landings took place at Besut, about eighty miles south of the Siamese border. The Japs from then on had complete command at sea and in the air.

After the departure northwards of the 12th Indian Infantry Brigade the 2nd Loyals (less B Company) was the only reserve in Fortress Command, which extended along the entire south coast of Singapore Island. The enemy bombed the airfield on 19 December, causing some casualties in the Battalion.

Gen Sir Archibald Wavell was made Supreme Commander, South-West Pacific, on 3 January, 1942, and four days later he ordered all allied forces to fall back on Johore. The retreat began on 10 January, the 8th and 11th Indian Divisions suffering heavy losses, so that Percival decided to send the 2nd Loyals by a train, which was held up for several reasons, to Segamat, about 102 miles from Singapore in north-central Johore; but his orders did not get through and, having suffered heavy air attack, Elrington was unable to reach his destination until 8.00 am on 13 December. From here on, interspersed by individual acts of gallantry which could not in themselves stem the overriding strength of the enemy, the Battalion retreated inch by inch to the final tragedy of Singapore.

Allied plans were completely thrown out by the invasion of the west coast of northern Johore on 16 January by a strong Japanese force at Muar. They advanced swiftly eastward up the Sungei Muar in an effort to cut off the retreating British, Australians, Indians and Malays. The 2nd Loyals were now under the command of the 27th Australian Infantry Brigade, and it was with the 2/30th Battalion, Australian Imperial Force, that the Loyals co-ordinated their retreat. Several times the two battalions, notably the Australians and HQ Company, beat off Japanese efforts to encircle them. The chief action took place on the northern outskirts of Ayer Hitam in central Johore where the essential problem was maintaining contact and a co-ordinated withdrawal. By 7.40 pm on 25 January, for example, the 2nd Loyals had been out of touch with their supporting artillery and the rear for nearly three hours. Shortly before telephone communication had broken down, Elrington had been told that his Battalion was to be withdrawn at dusk and sent back to Singapore by motor transport. The position was no longer tenable and the enemy were firing down the road, so that platoons had to make their way back through the marsh on either side of it. Although outflanked, C Company, under Capt P. Rogers, held on to its position with great determination, thus giving covering fire, while the rest of the Battalion crossed the river behind them, notwithstanding the fact that the bridge had then to be blown. This was boldly and successfully done, due in part to the stout defence by Capt Beattie's Company on the left flank, culminating in a spirited use of the bayonet.

With the Australians, and the 2nd Gordon Highlanders in support, the Loyals passed through the town and took up positions beyond it. From here they had motorized transport for some distance. Although reduced to twenty-three officers and 489 other ranks, the Battalion would have fared much worse had it not been for the initiative and high standard of bushcraft shown by groups and even individual soldiers. Typical was the skill shown by men of B Company on 23 January when Capt Leighton and Lts Wardle and Handley, with fifteen men, seeing the Company cut off, took to the jungle and decided to make for the Batu Pahat–Ayer Hitam road. They started off westwards, skirting the base of the Bukit Payong ridge, and after passing through a large rubber estate spent the night in the jungle.

But initiative and courage could not prevent the inevitable, and on 30 January Lt-Col Elrington received direct orders from HQ Malaya Command to take up a position covering the southern end of the Johore Causeway which connects Johore with Singapore Island. Next day the causeway was breached in two places.

On 1 February the Loyals were relieved at the causeway by 2/30th Australian Imperial Force and returned to Bidadari Camp, and that afternoon A Company with bren-gun carriers, under the command of Major F. G. Barnes, was detailed for internal security and the prevention of possible rioting by the indigenous people. At the same time Elrington took over command of the coast artillery and a machine-gun company of the Federated Malay States Volunteer Force, manning the Island's beach defences at Blakang Mati. Meanwhile, B Company and the amalgamated C and D Companies were to defend the unfortified northern shore of the island. All round, the 2nd Loyals had been given a formidable task.

On 5 February the islanders spotted, far out at sea, the blazing liner, the *Empress of Asia*, carrying, amongst her military passengers, the 18th Reconnaissance Battalion, formerly the 5th Loyals. Ten miles from the docks the liner was hit again by three bombs amidships. The casualties were heavy, but notable was the conduct of Lt-Col H. A. Fitt who, although badly burnt, displayed great courage in directing operations against low flying enemy aircraft and thereby inspiring all ranks. His bravery was later recognized by the award of the DSO. The survivors of the 18th Reconnaissance Battalion were duly taken off by HMS *Yarra* which drew alongside and, after re-equipment, the men were held in divisional reserve.

Three days later, on the evening of 8 February, two Japanese divisions made a surprise landing on the north-west shore of the island. The fundamental strategy was that of maintaining cohesion in the face of civilian, no less than military, demoralization. In this respect, the Loyals can look back with pride to their Second Battalion, the 18th Reconnaissance Battalion and to Brig Williams (the Regiment's penultimate Colonel) who did so much to secure liaison between British and Malay troops.

As the situation deteriorated the 2nd Loyals reverted to the command of the First Malayan Infantry Brigade and were given the task of stopping any enemy advance on the west coast approaches. The Japanese attacked repeatedly to gain vital points in the Ulu Pandan and Reformatory Road area. The 2nd Loyals' left flank on the higher and more open ground was protected by machine-gun sections of another unit until these were withdrawn without warning, thus allowing the Japs to get around the open flank.

To add to this predicament the 2nd Loyals found themselves fired upon from their rear. This caused consternation and casualties, but proved to be due to the mistaken zeal of inexperienced Indian troops sent up to strengthen the front line positions!

At approximately the same time the 18th Reconnaissance Battalion attacked Japanese positions astride the Bukit Timah road, and succeeded in establishing themselves in better defensive positions near the Singapore Racecourse. Confused fighting, sometimes with bayonets, took place after this, with considerable help from other units alongside (notably the British Battalion, an earlier amalgamation, on account of heavy losses, of the 2nd East Surreys and the 1st Royal Leicesters under Lt-Col C. E. Morrison, MC, of the Leicesters) until Friday 13 February, on which day the Admiralty oil tanks immediately to the rear of the 2nd Loyals' positions caught fire, and the First Malayan Infantry Brigade withdrew that night to the Alexandra Military Hospital–Gillman Barracks area. This withdrawal left the hospital without protection. On this day, too, the 18th Reconnaissance Battalion took up a new position in the Mt Pleasant Road area and, despite several fierce enemy attacks, was still unmoved when Singapore surrendered two days later.

The 2nd Loyals took up a carefully prepared position in the area of the Gillman Barracks (their peacetime home) and the Tiger Brewery. The nearby hospital was eventually captured by the enemy who shot or bayoneted those in the wards and even in the operating theatres. CD Company, under Capt Brooke, came under very heavy mortar fire in the bungalow area of the barracks, until eventually their strength was reduced to three officers and seventeen other ranks. Despite the gallantry of Major Leighton and his men, B Company also suffered severely. At one period the Company Commander used a bren-gun to such good effect that three times in quick succession the crews of a Jap field gun, firing over open sights, were knocked out. A composite company of B, C and D could muster only two rather thin platoons but HQ (Major Barnes) was still a respectable size,

11. *Men of the 47th at the Battle of Ali Masjid, 21 November, 1878*

12. *Men of the 2/5th Loyal North Lancashire Regiment wearing captured pickelhaube in Cambrai on 10 October, 1918*

13. *Major-Gen R. G. Kekewich*

14. *Lt W. A. Sandys-Clarke VC, the sixth member of his family to win the Victoria Cross*

15. *The North-West Frontier: the 1st Battalion, The Loyal Regiment, crossing the Tochi River in 1931*

16. The 1st Battalion, The Loyal Regiment, taking over Guard Duties in London from The Grenadier Guards in 1964

17. Field-Marshal Sir Gerald Templer presenting new colours to the 1st Battalion, The Queen's Lancashire Regiment, at Dover, 25 March, 1970 (from the painting by Terence Cuneo)

18. HM The Queen, as Colonel-in-Chief of the Loyal Regiment, arriving at Mercers' Hall with Brig G. A. Rimbault, the last Colonel of the Loyals, for the Regiment's last dinner in 1969

and was able to cover the withdrawal of their battered comrades to Mount Washington. At about 7.30 pm a light machine-gun section opened fire at some Japanese who appeared on high ground above Gillman Barracks. These were the last shots fired in the Malayan campaign. Again the Loyals had fought to the bitter end. Nearly an hour after Gen Percival had surrendered, this news had not yet reached the Battalion who were still preoccupied with the task to which they were called. All ranks were astounded by this development.

After initial concentration in Changi Gaol the 2nd Loyals were sent to Korea. The 18th Reconnaissance Battalion, however, was even more unfortunate, finding themselves after November, 1942, employed in building the infamous Burma Railway. Here Capt M. L. Webber and his twin brother operated a hidden radio set from which they were able to maintain some kind of morale by keeping the prisoners informed of the progress of the war. For this skilful and dangerous work Capt Webber was awarded the OBE. For his leadership of the 2nd Loyals in constantly difficult conditions Lt-Col Elrington perpetuated the military distinction of his family by receiving the DSO. At the end of the war he was also awarded an OBE for his equally distinguished, if less spectacular, leadership in various Japanese prisoner-of-war camps.

In active service and Japanese hands, the 2nd Loyals lost eight officers and 285 other ranks, and the 18th Reconnaissance Battalion (5th Loyals) twelve officers and 279 other ranks. These appalling losses show the extent to which the men of North Lancashire were involved in the worst defeat ever inflicted on the British Army and the bravery that was expected of them.

Following its withdrawal from Dunkirk and various postings in Britain, the 1st Loyals were able, at last, to hit back at the Germans as a result of 'Operation Torch', the Anglo-American landing in Algeria and Morocco under Gen Eisenhower which was designed to forge a link between these armies and Montgomery's Eighth Army which, since the second Battle of El

Alamein in October, 1942, had pursued Rommel's Afrika Korps westwards. The British in Algeria were under the command of Lt-Gen Sir Kenneth Anderson's First Army, and the Loyals, under Lt-Col G. W. Gibson, were still in the Second Brigade (Brig E. E. J. Moore) of the First Division (Major-Gen W. E. Clutter-buck). The Loyals reached Algiers in the *Duchess of York* on 9 March, 1943.

The Division had not been in the initial landing the previous autumn, but was sent to reinforce the First Army in its determined efforts to capture Medjez-el-Bab, on the southern approaches to Tunis, which the Germans under Gen von Arnim were tenaciously holding. Veterans of the Tunisian campaign will recall particularly the struggle for the salient at Medjez-el-Bab, which (as the word means) is a gateway and was the pivot on which hinged the Germans' last desperate defence of Tunis. Thereafter, particularly, will be recalled the battles of Mac-gregor Hill, The Basin, Gueriat-el-Atach and Gabgab Gap, before the enemy fell back on the capital.

The Brigade's comradeship was to take them through North Africa, the bloodless victory of Pantellaria, into Italy, on to the beaches of Anzio and beyond, and finally to victory. Firstly, then, Medjez: the Loyals' assignment here was to hold the apex of a salient which the enemy had driven four miles south-east of the town, to a position which the Battalion took over from the 2nd Lancashire Fusiliers on 24 March. This took them into the area of a feature known as The Basin, around which the Loyals were deployed mostly in the north and east. Two miles to the east the Fourth Division was deployed in an easterly direction, and providing the anvil on which the hammer of the Eighth Army would be struck. After Macgregor Hill and The Basin had been cleared of an enemy which used every weapon (particu-larly mines) to hold the British, the Second Brigade's advance took them northward, across the road between Medjez and Peter's Corner. The Loyals provided the western arm of the Brigade, sharing the toughest fighting with the 1st North Stafford-shire to their east and the 6th Gordons beyond them – all batta-lions up. To the north-west of the Loyals was the 24th Guards

Brigade and, beyond them over the vital arm of the Medjerda River downstream from Medjez, the 78th Division.

Particularly hard hit on this feature was C Company of the Loyals, on the north-west flank. At the juncture with the North Staffords, astride the road from Snake Ridge to Montarnaud, was B Company to which belonged the Regiment's sole recipient of the Victoria Cross during the Second World War – a war in which that decoration was so rare that no less a person than Gen Horrocks has written that not one recommendation he had made in XXX Corps had been accepted. The author also understands that offensive action, rather than acts of bravery in rescuing wounded comrades under fire, was more favourably considered. This VC certainly contained that ingredient. Already the Battalion had suffered heavy casualties, which included the death of Lt-Col Gibson from whom command devolved eventually to Lt-Col Fulbrook who had been in the Regiment for thirty years, serving in every rank from drummer upwards and who was to win the DSO for his fine leadership.

Lt W. A. Sandys-Clarke was the only surviving officer of B Company. He had been wounded in the neck and hand by splinters and had had his wounds hurriedly dressed, although it was thought that a head wound had upset his judgement and made him reckless. Certain that he could retake his Company's objective he applied, on 23 April, for his Commanding Officer's permission to collect about twenty men at Battalion HQ and he duly set off with them towards the German positions. Progress was good in the early stages, before they were pinned down by machine-gun fire. Arranging for his men to give him covering fire Sandys-Clarke tackled the first post single-handed and knocked out the enemy gun. Held up again by two more machine-guns he reported to Col Fulbrook that he could go no further. After taking advice to use battle drill, Sandys-Clarke again arranged for action. Finally, he led his men on to their last position on the far side of Gueriat-el-Atach. But whilst consolidating his gain his men came under renewed sniper fire. Again this gallant young officer tackled the enemy snipers alone, and was only a few feet away from the enemy when he was killed.

In the words of the citation for his posthumous Victoria Cross, he had shown a 'quick grasp of the situation, whilst his outstanding personal bravery and tenacious devotion to duty were an inspiration to his company, and were beyond praise'.

But Gueriat-el-Atach was not yet taken, and it was with the help of the 1st Duke of Wellington's Regiment that the depleted Loyals at last won control. Many officers and men had shown great bravery and several decorations were won. Of the thirty-three officers and 801 other ranks who had constituted the 1st Loyals on 1st April, only fourteen officers and 520 men remained.

But German resistance did not diminish, and all witnesses of the remaining campaign will testify that during the last ten days of April it became almost fanatical. For the Loyals this meant chiefly the Battle for Gabgab Gap, through which passed the road from the link between Medjez and Tunis to Montarnaud. Here the Germans made extensive use of tanks which they poured in from the north-west and dug in so that they became difficult to sight and remove, known as hull down positions. The Loyals, no less than the Germans and other allied units, continued to lose heavily. But Gen Alexander now cut off the Bon Peninsula, a master-stroke which presaged the capture of Tunis on 13 May, 1943. Not only bells of rejoicing, but a single funereal bell rang out over Tunis for those who had fallen against a determined foe, and a memorial tablet was afterwards placed in St George's Church in Tunis. Addressing his Division, Major-Gen Clutterbuck reminded them that they had borne 'the brunt of the fighting in the final battle for Tunis – and let nobody forget it'. The war in North Africa was over.

After a brief and bloodless victory over the imminently surrendering Italians on the island of Pantellaria, the Second Brigade was withdrawn to Bizerta. Meanwhile, 'Operation Huskey' initiated the seizure of Sicily which was completed in a mere six weeks by American troops, relying, to find their modern fighting feet, on the British 78th Division, now transferred to Gen Montgomery's Eighth Army. The British First Division's turn was to come next, at the end of November, 1943, when Gen Alexander's combined Army Group in Italy, consisting of the British Eighth Army under Lt-Gen Sir Oliver Leese and the American Fifth Army under Lt-Gen Mark Clark, was struggling to take the German 'Gustav Line', particularly near Cassino at the junction of the two armies. Thus Alexander decided to turn the enemy's flank by landing fresh forces in an amphibious operation at Anzio, namely the British First Division, under Major-Gen Penney, and the American Third Division, under Major-Gen Truscott. And so came the legendary struggle – a battle not surpassed for ferocity in the entire history of The Loyal Regiment. By adopting this strategy Alexander hoped to speed the drive on Rome and remove the pressure on the sorely tried allies at Cassino.

Landing first at Taranto, the Battalion concentrated in Eighth Army area, but later moved across the Apennines to Salerno where the amphibious landing was rehearsed.

In the early hours of 22 January the Second Infantry Brigade landed as planned on 'Peter Beach', six miles north-west of Anzio and achieved local tactical surprise. The 1st Loyals had been allotted the extreme left flank of the allied landing, an area of great importance where an enemy counter-attack was thought to be most likely. South of the port of Anzio the Americans achieved equal success and by the afternoon all objectives had been captured.

The expedition, of corps strength, was commanded by Lt-Gen Lucas, a friendly, 'folksy' American who smoked a corn-cob pipe. Initially he led it with success but, failing to take advantage of the initial surprise achieved, he held back the advance until he was certain that his armour was fully ashore and he could meet any German onslaught or counter-thrust. And so it was not until 25 January that the 24th Guards Brigade was allowed to advance from the initial beachhead, when they captured Carroceto, some eight miles up the Anzio–Rome road. Here they ran into strong opposition, while on the southern flank the Americans were held up three miles short of Cisterna. The Germans had taken full advantage of the breathing space given to them and had swiftly concentrated their forces. Hitler had ordered Field-Marshal von Kesselring 'to remove the abscess south of Rome' and Gen von

Mackensen, the enemy commander on the spot, struck swiftly and powerfully to achieve this. Efforts by the First British Division and the Third United States Division to resume the beachhead were halted with heavy losses and soon the allies were fighting desperately on the defensive.

During the first two weeks of February the Germans, bringing up more and more reinforcements, regained Carroceto and the Buonriposo Ridge, and on 17 February broke through the Americans holding part of the line in front of the 1st Loyals who were in reserve. The Battalion position ran east for about a mile from the Flyover Bridge, a modern bridge of the kind which Mussolini had built so plentifully to facilitate Italian transport before the war, spanning the main Anzio–Rome road and railway. For every veteran of the Loyals this name stands out as the scene of the hardest fighting in the whole of the Italian campaign. This was the 'last ditch' position of the whole Allied beachhead. If the Germans succeeded in breaking through the Flyover position there was nothing to stop them sweeping down to the port of Anzio.

The first German attack began at 10.30 pm on 17 February. The shelling on both sides was tremendous, for the Germans tried to blast a way through for their assault, while the British artillery were firing continuous SOS tasks and hammering away at the suspected German forming-up areas. Early on the morning of the 18th B Company bore the brunt of a determined assault in which many men and all the officers became casualties. CSM Moran played an outstanding part in reorganizing the survivors and was later awarded the MM. The Germans, however, had succeeded in gaining a foothold in B Company's area and followed up with a fresh attack on A Company, nearest the bridge. Major Maher, CSM Duffy and many men were killed, but Capt Knowles and Lt Winn brilliantly maintained the defence and forced the Germans to withdraw, leaving large numbers of killed and wounded in front of the Company position.

Later in the day Lt-Col Fulbrook launched D Company with the Carrier Platoon on foot in a counter-attack to clear the Germans from B Company area. Splendidly led by Major

Abramovich, this counter-attack was completely successful and ten prisoners were captured. By dark the Battalion area was reorganized. During a lull Major Rimbault took over command from Lt-Col Fulbrook whose last day had been outstandingly successful.

Enemy shelling and patrolling throughout the night and a German dive-bombing attack heralded a strong assault soon after dawn against C Company and part of B Company. Casualties were again heavy, and C Company HQ and two platoons were overrun. However 15 Platoon under Lt Black hung doggedly to their positions until the end of the battle.

With the remnants of all four rifle companies in forward positions the Brigade Commander gave Lt-Col Rimbault a company of the 2nd North Staffords with which to stage a counter-attack Supported by three tanks and the Mortar Platoon of the Loyals this attack was the turning point of the battle, for the Germans, who had fought so fiercely, suddenly crumpled. As Wynford Vaughan-Thomas wrote in *Anzio*, 'The Loyals, worn but with pride in their hearts, saw a sight which they had hardly dared to hope they might see on the Beachhead – their enemies were retreating . . .' D Company joined the North Staffs Company in mopping up and 200 prisoners were taken.

Indeed, casualties on both sides were appalling, and the Loyals had sustained their heaviest losses of the war, second only to the Gordon Highlanders at Anzio. Even Gen Penney had been wounded and during the last stage of the battle First and Fifty-Sixth Divisions were commanded jointly by Major-Gen Templer, an old comrade-in-arms of the Loyals.

For the next two-and-a-half months a period of static warfare followed along the Anzio beachhead. The Second Infantry Brigade's front of about 3,500 yards was divided into two. The 1st Loyals were entrusted with the left-hand sector, their old battle ground including the bridge and the lateral road, Wigan Street. On the right of the Brigade was the 45th US Division with whom the British troops worked in the closest harmony.

With the advent of the drier spring weather the defences were improved until the trench systems resembled those of the First

World War, and patrolling at night was continuous. In this period, to quote the First Divisional History, 'the Second Infantry Brigade patrols gradually acquired an ascendancy over the enemy'. A notable success was achieved by Capt J. F. Winn who led a patrol into the German lines, lay concealed all day and in the evening extracted two prisoners from an enemy trench and returned safely. For his fine leadership during this period Capt Winn was awarded the unusual distinction of an American Silver Star, to which was later added the MC at Florence. That he should have won this United States decoration indicates how closely the armies worked together.

On 11 May, Gen Alexander launched a strong offensive on the Cassino front and a fortnight later American troops, advancing up the west coast, linked up with an Anglo-American column which broke out from the beachhead. At long last the Anzio garrison, now under Gen L. K. Truscott, went over to the offensive. Cisterna fell to the Americans on 25 May and on the 28th the First Division (now commanded by Brig C. F. Loewen) recaptured Carroceto and advanced to the line of the River Moletta. On 29 May the axis of advance was switched to the north-west and the 1st Loyals advanced to the area of the Ardea–Campoleone road. On 31 May what proved to be the final assault of the campaign was launched against the German rearguards, who resisted bravely. Lt-Col Rimbault was wounded in this action and command devolved upon Major J. D. Robbins who had earlier joined the Battalion from the 2/7th Middlesex. He organized the final assault and led the Battalion to the outskirts of Rome, where the First Division was pulled out of the line for a well-earned rest.

So heavy had been the casualties that the Battle of Anzio was almost a Pyrrhic victory for the Allies, although the overall strategy had been achieved. Since the landing on 22 January the 1st Loyals had suffered the death of six officers and eighty-five other ranks, and the wounding of twenty-one officers and 341 other ranks. But, in Italy overall, other battalions in the Division had suffered even worse casualties. On the last day of June a ceremonial parade was held in Rome where the divisional commander, Major-Gen Penney, now recovered from his wounds, thanked the Loyals for their part in the victory. Only the day after the occupation of Rome (which, because of its antiquity, the enemy did not defend) the Allies landed on the beaches of Normandy. But the Battle of Anzio had had catastrophic results on the enemy, however gallantly they had defended the beach-head, for it required the removal to Italy of ten divisions which were urgently needed in northern France, over eight hundred miles away. Gen Penney was also correct when he reminded his men, quite simply, 'No Anzio, no Rome'.

Against Churchill's wishes, the swift seizure of Hitler's next line of defence (the Gothic Line which ran across northern Italy from the Tuscan Archipelago to just south of Rimini) was prevented by America's wish to place priority on the invasion of southern France, which slowed down the impetus of the allied offensive.

At the end of July the Loyals were visited by King George VI, and Lt-Col Rimbault was presented to His Majesty. On the 30th of the month the strength of the Battalion stood at 730 all ranks, which included a draft from other regiments, for the losses at Anzio had been heavy.

The 1st Loyals were now transferred to Lt-Gen Kirkman's XIII Corps for its next great offensive – the capture of the hilly country around Florence, for which task the Corps itself was transferred from the Eighth to the Fifth Army. The Battalion took over a sector of the front from the 1/6th East Surreys, but instead of attacking divisionally across the River Arno on the Villamagua sector they were moved to the north-east portion of Florence which, like Rome, was declared an open city.

Fighting broke out at Fiesole. A successful patrol led by Lt A. J. Dymond and an erroneous report from a neighbouring unit that the Germans were withdrawing led the Brigade Commander, now Brig C. E. A. Firth, to order the 1st Loyals to seize the Fiesole Ridge without artillery support. This ridge is very steep and difficult to climb, as the slopes are intersected by the walls and terraces of many beautiful villas. A Company (Major G. W. Croker) and B Company (Major J. F. Winn) advanced up the ridge but soon ran into fierce resistance, the Germans using well-concealed machine guns and mortars. Both companies bravely forced their way up the hill and across the road that runs diagonally to the summit. The greatest difficulty was experienced in getting the wounded back over the walls and terraces, and many brave deeds were performed. Winn, Croker and Dymond all won the MC and Sgt Todhunter, who had carried a severely wounded man to safety whilst himself wounded, received the DCM. MMs went to Sgt Rawlinson, Cpl Taylor, L/Cpl Walmsley and to L/Cpl Spencer who had continued to work his wireless set whilst wounded in both arms. Heavy fighting persisted in the area of the ridge, but the whole district was eventually captured by a detour.

The Battalion continued by many acts of courage to push its way up the Appenines, through such twisting roads as Arrow Route, until it reached its final action in Italy in the defence of Monte Grande, five miles west of the Plain of Lombardy. Monte Grande had formed the apex of a salient on the American front, exposed on three sides, and during the bitter winter of 1944–45, facing fierce German resistance, our allies suffered heavy casualties. On 4 November the Loyals duly relieved the 350th RCT (Regimental Combat Team, which is of about equal strength to a British infantry brigade) on top of Monte Grande, and it will always be to the credit of the Second Brigade that this feature was held despite constant shelling, the positions being exchanged between the Loyals, the North Staffords and the Gordons during the following weeks.

On 27 January, 1945, the Brigade left for Palestine, via Perugia; but Monte Grande was still to be occupied by The Loyal Regiment, for the newly-formed Second Battalion (now ironically under a Jewish Brigade), created from the 10th, which had already seen service at San Clemente, duly took over the hill feature, whilst the Germans still occupied the northern side. But again the enemy was eventually forced to withdraw by the threat of encirclement. Bologna was captured on 21 April and the battle rolled northward until news came of the German surrender on 2 May.

Thus far for the infanteered Loyals: the 7th Battalion, raised in 1940, was converted in 1941 to the 92nd (Loyals) LAA Regiment (Lt-Col P. R. Henderson, RA). It landed in France on D-Day with the Third Division and served with great distinction until the end of the war.

The Loyals were also represented in North-West Europe by the 8th Battalion, raised at the same time, which became the 93rd (Loyals) LAA Regiment, RA (Lt-Col W. Odling). These regiments particularly distinguished themselves at the crossing of the Rhine, as the 92nd had done on the Orne.

The 9th Battalion was formed in 1940 under the command of Lt-Col B. O. Ware. In the following year it was converted into the 148th Battalion, RAC, and equipped with Churchill tanks. In 1944 the Battalion, by then commanded by Lt-Col R. G. Cracroft, MC, of the RAC, took part in the ferocious battle of Caen. Unfortunately the CO was amongst a number of officers and men killed in this action. Later in 1944 the Royal Armoured Corps was reorganized and the 148th Battalion was dispersed to other armoured units.

Meanwhile, the 6th Loyals, a TA battalion, added to the Regiment's reputation for ubiquity by serving in Burma. Raised in 1939 it was converted in 1941 to the 2nd Regiment, the Reconnaissance Corps. In 1942 it sailed for India with the Second Division, and after service in Assam moved to Burma in 1944–45 where, at one stage after the capture of Imphal, it advanced ninety miles in two days. Lt-Col Bradford, who had led the Regiment with such efficiency, was promoted on 22 June, 1945, to become second-in-command of an Indian Infantry Brigade. The Regiment was disbanded on its return to England in November, 1945.

The Second World War had cost The Loyal Regiment the lives of seventy officers and 1,137 other ranks. Though not as atrocious as the First World War, that figure, by the standards of the conflicts between 1939 and 1945, speaks for itself; and it is one which the Loyals regard both with grief and pride.

CHAPTER 15

Into the Atomic Age

T HAT the Loyals survived longer than any other regiment
which was eventually to be amalgamated testified to the
high regard in which they were held by the War Office and
the Ministry of Defence. Only a handful of line regiments survived the final regrouping. But although the Loyals, the last
Lancashire Regiment to lose its old identity, should eventually
disappear, it was only logical that the numerous regiments of the
thickly populated County of Lancaster should eventually form
a single regiment. Thus the Corps first associated with Lancashire,
when in 1782 the 47th established a depôt at Preston and became
known as The Lancashire Regiment, was the last to disappear;
although it was junior in the Army to several regiments which
subsequently became associated with Lancashire.

Undoubtedly, one of the reasons for the Loyals' survival until
1970 was that they had been selected for so many important tasks
after the War. They were to serve in Palestine, Eritrea, Trieste,
Malaya, Swaziland and Aden before bowing out; although no
regiment believes that it has vanished, but simply that its spirit
survives in a new and unified command.

Perhaps the two most taxing of the Regiment's post-war duties
were in Palestine and Malaya, theatres of operation in which the
Loyals had already served honourably but without much sense
of nostalgia. First, then, Palestine; in fact, Palestine and the
Levant (now Lebanon). The 1st Loyals, under Lt-Col G. A.
Rimbault, DSO, MC, went straight from a year's hard fighting
in Italy to southern Palestine where, during the last weeks of the
war, it was intended that they should rest, reorganize and train.
Sailing from Taranto, they reached Haifa on 5 February, 1945,
and moved to tented accommodation thirteen miles north of Gaza.
They were required to be ready to send a mobile column of two

companies to Jerusalem, if needed, and to keep order in Jaffa and Tel Aviv which were separated only by a wire barricade.

By November the situation had deteriorated as the Irgun Zvai Leumi and the Stern Gang organized Jewish resistance against the British whom they regarded as inhibiting their efforts to claim Palestine for their own people. Detecting and tracking down the terrorists was an exercise with which the Loyals had become familiar. A successful operation of this nature was carried out by the Loyals and the 2/7th Middlesex when they captured some terrorists who had blown up the coastguard station near Athlit.

Later, when the Battalion took part in house-to-house fighting – an operation which went on continuously for four days and nights – the Loyals succeeded in capturing the most notorious member of the Stern Gang. During an attempt by the Jews to disembark a shipload of illegal immigrants at Haifa, a mob attempted to storm the docks. The situation was quelled by Major J. F. Winn whose prompt action in ordering B Company to open controlled fire quickly cleared the streets and acted as a salutary lesson to all concerned.

In February, 1947, the Battalion moved to Eritrea under the command of Lt-Col J. W. E. R. Gainher, OBE; but again they were committed to action against terrorists and brigands, their opponents being the Shuftas. With battalions of three other infantry regiments, armoured cars of the 15/19th Hussars and local Sudanese units, they found this an exacting task in wild, torrid country beside the Red Sea. The next year the Battalion went to Mogadishu in Italian Somaliland where, like The East Surrey Regiment and others, it was involved in the administration of that territory after Italy's defeat in order to facilitate the eventual handing over of power to the Somalis.

In 1949 the Battalion sailed for Cyprus where Lt-Col R. V. Boyle assumed command. Here, on 12 March, the First and Second Battalions – the old 47th and 81st – were amalgamated at a parade in Nicosia, in the presence of Field-Marshal Sir William Slim, the Chief of the Imperial General Staff. Nearly every infantry regiment of the line suffered similarly at about this time; the shrinkage of the British Army had begun. Henceforth, there was to be only one regular battalion of the Regiment – the 1st Loyals. Mordaunt and Bertie had joined forces at last!

The following year found the new battalion in the Canal Zone, under the command of Lt-Col M. P. Huthwaite, serving in the important strategic port of Aqaba. A rather longer period was served here before, in the Coronation year of 1953, the Loyals went to Trieste, that seaport disputed for so long between Italy and Yugoslavia where military diplomacy of the highest order was required. The Battalion was there until Britain's final evacuation the following year, when Lt-Col J. W. A. Stares, DSO, OBE, assumed command. A treaty was eventually signed in London, returning Trieste to Italy, and on 25 October, 1954, the Italian Army arrived to take the frontier posts over from the Loyals; and Rozetti Barracks, Trieste, from the reborn 2nd Lancashire Fusiliers.

Now came perhaps the Loyals' last great military achievement. After a few years in England the Battalion sailed in January, 1957, for three years' service in Malaya from which, this time, they were to return as victors. The Regiment had arrived in Malaya to hold the line which was represented by seven battalions. Soon afterwards there arrived an eighth – the 22nd Special Air Service Regiment. The Royal Armoured Corps also had two farflung regiments in the bush. Mr Frank Allen, a journalist on the *Bolton Journal and Guardian*, was sent out to Malaya to despatch a series of articles to his newspaper, a task which he did admirably. He finished the Preface to a bound edition of these articles by writing: 'Soldiers are notably poor correspondents. They always forget to tell their parents and relations those things which they want most to know. Perhaps these articles will supply some of the omissions and assure parents that their boys are doing a worthwhile job in Malaya and doing it well.' Allen emphasized particularly the splendid liaison and co-operation in the Battalion under its Commanding Officer, Lt-Col C. L. Thompson, in constantly difficult conditions, and the excellent relations which the men struck up with the native trackers who were frequently able to guide them on to their objectives. Col Thompson was made an OBE for his outstanding work in this campaign. The Loyals was the last of the old regiments to leave Malaya, under the command of the Commonwealth Brigade, in December, 1959. On its departure Gen (later Field-Marshal) Sir Francis Festing told the men: 'Your record of seventeen CTs (Communist terrorists) killed and two captured during your first two years of operations is one that has not been equalled in your brigade or elsewhere in recent times.' The Loyals were followed by what, at the time, sounded like an extraordinary regimental amalgam, the 1/3rd East Anglian Regiment.

Climatically, the Loyals must have felt a sharp chill because, returning home in January, 1960, they were sent almost at once to Wuppertal in Germany. There they remained for about two years under the command of Lt-Col D. E. Crawley, MC, an officer who had greatly distinguished himself whilst serving with The Parachute Regiment at Arnhem, before enjoying another brief glance at their own country, for they were stationed at Barnard Castle in March, 1962. The following year came an assignment which, although the terror there was well past its worst, was still regarded with some dread – Cyprus. The tour was short, and in the summer of 1963 came an unusual posting – this time to Swaziland where, among other duties, the Battalion found the Guard of Honour on the departure of His Excellency the Queen's Commissioner, Sir Brian Marwick, at Mbabane. The men were home in time for Christmas.

The Regiment's last overseas posting was not as a whole unit, but only of company strength. When the situation in Borneo had been settled, there remained only one colonial problem which required military assistance. Excepting the ever-menacing and not altogether similar situation on our own doorstep, none would doubt that Aden was Britain's last colonial war, and, albeit of only company strength, the Loyals were to be present when the curtain went down on the Imperial stage. The protagonists who vied with each other in their attempt to rid Aden of the British were the 'National Liberation Front', known as the NLF, and the less aggressive FLOSY (or Flosy) which was openly backed by Egypt. To cope with this the Aden Brigade was increased to four battalions at the beginning of the most turbulent year, 1967. The

Loyals were at that time stationed in Malta under the command of Lt-Col M. H. H. Collins, OBE, the son of Lt-Col Neville Collins who had taken the First Battalion to France in 1939. Family succession in the Regiment has always been a noticeable trait, deriving from both the 47th and the 81st. The Loyals was one of four regiments who sent single companies, in addition to several whole battalions of others, to patrol such unpleasant districts as Crater and Maalla. Thus the Regiment was represented at our last serious colonial commitment. The Middle East had always been a stamping ground for The Loyal Regiment and its forbears.

So much for the Regiment's active service since the Second World War. Within a few years of the war its distinction was duly recognized in a variety of ways. On 7 October, 1949, new Colours were presented to the First Battalion on behalf of King George VI by Gen Sir John Crocker, GCB, KBE, DSO, MC, ADC, whilst it was stationed at Famagusta in Cyprus. Three years later came the Civic Honour, which surely epitomizes the strong bond between a regiment and the civilian population from which it has traditionally drawn its strength. This honour was conferred upon The Loyal Regiment with full pageantry at a special Ceremony of Adoption by the City of Preston on 6 September, 1952, when a magnificent scroll, enclosed in a silver casket, was presented to the Regiment. The special meeting to decide on the adoption was held on 7 August, a fact recorded, *inter alia*, on the scroll, at the top of which are the Queen's and Regimental Colours and, on the right-hand side, the Regiment's Battle Honours prior to 1914.

Of great pride to The Loyal Regiment was its Royal connection, for on 1 June, 1953, the day before her Coronation, Her Majesty the Queen graciously assumed the appointment of Colonel-in-Chief of the Regiment – an honour shared by only two other Line regiments. The following year the Regiment presented the Queen with a regimental badge in the form of a jewelled brooch, the presentation being performed at Buckingham Palace by a delegation consisting of the Colonel of the Regiment, Brig G. G. R. Williams, MBE, the Commanding Officer of the First Battalion, Lt-Col J. W. A. Stares, DSO, OBE, and the

Commanding Officer of the Depôt, Major J. C. Johnson. Two years later, on 4 June, 1956, the Queen, as Colonel-in-Chief, accompanied by Prince Philip, reviewed the First Battalion at Stockton Racecourse and congratulated the officers and men on their fine turn-out and drill.

But Royal Ceremonial did not end there. At the end of July, 1964, The Loyal Regiment took over Public Duties in London from The Grenadier Guards. These duties included the mounting of guards at Buckingham Palace, St James's Palace and the Tower of London and finding the Bank of England Picquet. This was a great honour for a Regiment of the Line and one which the Regiment performed meticulously in the evening of its life.

One other memorable event must be recorded before we come to the end of the story. The amalgamation of The Loyal Regiment with The Lancashire Regiment (PWV) had been ordered for 1970, so it was clear that 1969 would be the last Regimental Dinner for the Officers of the 47th/81st Dinner Club. Her Majesty the Queen, as Colonel-in-Chief of the Regiment, graciously accepted an invitation to dine with her officers and their ladies in the Hall of The Mercers' Company, the senior of the Livery Companies of London. It was an occasion of splendour during which the Queen, for nearly an hour, moved around the room, talking informally to all.

The actual amalgamation parade took place on 25 March, 1970, at Dover on a day of heavy cloud and savage cold. For many years Field-Marshal Templer had, at various times, been associated with The Loyal Regiment, and it was appropriate that The Queen's Lancashire Regiment should have been ushered in under his auspices. For the last time the Colonels of the two old Regiments inspected their Battalions, and their Colours were marched off. The new Regiment was formed under the command of Lt-Col D. Houston, the last Commanding Officer of the Loyals, and the Field-Marshal presented the new Colours and addressed the parade in memorable words.

Regiments will die, as they are born, at the call of necessity; and however much this is to be regretted, it was a decision which followed two-and-a-half centuries of firm decisions and devoted service to Crown and Country.

E

Epilogue

by Brigadier G. A. Rimbault, CBE, DSO, MC, DL
The last Colonel of The Loyal Regiment (North Lancashire)

Quebec, Maida, Corunna, Inkerman, Kimberley, Mons, Ypres, Gaza, Kilimanjaro, Dunkirk, North Africa, Anzio – the names record a story of honourable service to the Crown of England. And how brilliantly Michael Langley has written that story in this admirable history of the Regiment. How I wish that such a concise and readable history had been available to me when I was first commissioned and needed a balanced picture of all the great deeds of the past. We offer him our congratulations and our sincere thanks.

In 1958 the size of the Regular Army was greatly reduced, and in the Infantry the reduction was achieved by a series of amalgamations. In the north-west of England The King's Own Royal Regiment was amalgamated with The Border Regiment, The King's Regiment (Liverpool) with The Manchester Regiment and The East Lancashire Regiment with The South Lancashire Regiment (Prince of Wales's Volunteers). The Loyal Regiment was left untouched, and remained so for a further twelve years.

However, in 1970 further reductions were ordered, and the Loyals were amalgamated with The Lancashire Regiment (PWV) – old friends and neighbours – to form The Queen's Lancashire Regiment. Her Majesty Queen Elizabeth II, who had become Colonel-in-Chief of The Loyal Regiment in 1953, graciously consented to become Colonel-in-Chief of The Queen's Lancashires.

So today The Loyal Regiment has ceased to exist as a Regiment of the Regular British Army, but its spirit lives on in the ranks of The Queen's Lancashire Regiment.

The spirit of the Regiment is something that cannot easily be explained in words. It can only be fully understood by someone who has served with it, especially in battle. It is that magical power that makes a soldier go on when he has reached the limit of his ordinary capability. It was the spirit of The Loyal Regiment that enabled the 2nd Battalion to fight to the end in Singapore and to endure the terrible years that followed and emerge unbowed at the end. It was the spirit of the Regiment that carried the 1st Battalion to the summit of that bitterly contested North African ridge known as Gueriat-el-Atach and later enabled it to triumph against great odds at the Flyover Bridge at Anzio.

It was an honour to have been a 'Loyal'.

Loyauté M'Oblige.

APPENDIX A

Important Dates in the History of The Loyal Regiment

1741	Raising of what became the 47th (numbered in 1751) by Major-Gen John Mordaunt, by Royal command.
1745	47th as part of Sir William Cope's army which was defeated in Scotland, notably at Prestonpans (ironically named!).
1751	Numerical precedence supersedes identity of regiments by colonels' names.
1756	Outbreak of The Seven Years' War.
1758	47th Regiment's first battle honour at Louisburg. Nova Scotia finally captured from the French. Lascelle's Regiment (47th) closely involved.
1759	47th Regiment in the victorious Battle of Quebec. They became known as 'Wolfe's Own' and held a position in the centre of the Line, near Wolfe's Headquarters.
1775–1783	The 47th fought on several fronts in the war of American Independence. Present at Lexington, Bunker's Hill and Saratoga.
1782	The 47th became the first regiment to be associated with the County of Lancaster (The Lancashire Regiment). A depôt established at Preston. British regiments take on secondary titles.
1793	In response to the French Revolutionary Wars Major-Gen Albemarle Bertie was commanded to raise a Regiment of Infantry which became the 81st Foot, or The Loyal Lincoln Volunteers—a title which was formally recognized in 1832.
1793–1797	The 81st took a notable part in the French Revolutionary Wars, suffering heavily from yellow fever in the West Indies.
1797–1798	81st served in Guernsey during Napoleonic threat.
1799–1802	The 81st served in South Africa, and had an uncomfortable war against both Boers and Zulus.
1802	The Peace of Amiens brought temporary truce. The 81st strengthened the 22nd (later The Cheshire Regiment) in India; remainder returned to Britain.

114

1806	4 July: 1/81st took a major part in inflicting the first defeat on Napoleonic forces in Europe at Maida.
1806–1807	1/47th in the inglorious campaign against the Spanish in South America.
1807	Treaty of Tilsit temporarily allies France with Russia. The 1/47th served with distinction to quell Franco-Russian inspired risings in the Persian Gulf.
1808–1809	2/81st in Sir John Moore's gallant retreat to Corunna.
1809	2/81st sustained heavy losses owing to malaria on Walcheren Island.
1809–1813	2/47th in Spain. Major victory at Tarifa; the Regiment helped to pursue the French to the Pyrenees and were present at many notable engagements, including Vittoria.
1810–1811	1/47th and 65th restore peace in the Rann of Kutch.
1817–1818	47th and 65th achieved outstanding success in the Mahratta (or Pindari) Wars, one of the largest campaigns ever conducted in India.
1824–1826	47th quelled rising in Burma and won battle honour, 'Ava'.
1832	The 47th Foot took on the subsidiary title, The Lancashire Regiment; the 81st became The Loyal Lincoln Volunteers (both titles hitherto informal).
1854–1856	47th distinguished itself in the Crimean War; was present on the Alma and at Inkerman and Sevastopol. Regiment's first VC won at Inkerman.
1857	81st quelled incipient rising among the Sepoys at Lahore and elsewhere in the Punjab during the Indian Mutiny.
1873	All regiments above the 25th Foot paired for alternate service abroad (mostly in India) and at home. 81st paired with 47th.
1878–1879	81st in Second Afghan War: won the important battle at Ali Masjid.
1881	Cardwell's Army Reforms: Purchase system abolished; replacement of old numerical precedence with county titles, hence 1782 names also scrapped. Henceforth the 47th and 81st became the 1st and 2nd Battalions, The Loyal North Lancashire Regiment.
1899–1902	The Boer War. The 2nd Loyal North Lancs, under Lt-Col Kekewich held Kimberley against a long siege by the Boers. The Battalion was also active elsewhere on the western sector of the Boers' front.
1914–1918	The First World War. The Loyal North Lancs raised 21 battalions and fought on practically every front. The Regiment won 68 battle honours and 3 VCs, but sus-

tained the deaths of 357 officers and 7,232 other ranks.

1919–1939   The 1st Battalion served in Ireland, at Chanak, in North China, Calcutta, the North-West Frontier and Palestine; the 2nd Battalion served in Shanghai and sailed thence to Singapore where they were stationed when the Japanese invaded.

1921   The Regiment became known as The Loyal Regiment.

1939–1945   The Second World War. The Loyal Regiment fought on every front. The 1st Battalion was the last to leave Dunkirk; the 2nd Battalion (re-formed to fight in Italy) surrendered at Singapore. 4 Territorial Battalions on active service. Regiment won 21 battle honours and 1 VC, but sustained the deaths of 70 officers and 1,137 other ranks.

1945–1970   The Regiment served in Palestine, Eritrea, Trieste, Malaya, Swaziland and sent a company to Aden.

1949   The 1st and 2nd Battalions amalgamated in Cyprus.

1952   Adoption of The Loyal Regiment by the town of Preston.

1953   HM Queen Elizabeth II became Colonel-in-Chief of The Loyal Regiment.

1964   July–August: the Regiment performed Ceremonial Duties in London.

1970   On 25 March The Loyal Regiment (the last Lancashire regiment to lose its identity) was amalgamated with The Lancashire Regiment, and became the 1st Battalion The Queen's Lancashire Regiment, of which the Queen is Colonel-in-Chief.

APPENDIX B

The Regimental March

The Regimental Quick March of the 47th was *The Mountain Rose*, a traditional air, probably of French origin. The date of its adoption is unknown, although it had been the Regimental March of The Bedfordshire Regiment until 1882.

The 47th Slow March has no name, although it resembles *The Mountain Rose*.

The 81st Regimental Quick March was *The Lincolnshire Poacher*, believed to have been adopted in 1820. The 81st did not have a Slow March.

The 4th Loyals Quick March before 1907 was *Sally Come Up*, a tune of unknown origin and adoption; whilst the 5th Loyals' Quick March was *Stanley For Ever*, a tune by an unrecorded composer marking the close connection between the Regiment and the Earls of Derby.

The Loyal North Lancashire Regiment Quick March, *The Red, Red Rose*, is based on an old Scottish air, *Down in the Broom*. It was adopted by both Regular Battalions, on War Office instructions, in about 1885; and by the 3rd, 4th and 5th Battalions in 1907. The Red Rose conveniently refers to that of Lancashire, but the words are by Robert Burns which is appropriate in view of the Regiment's original association with Scotland. The score is as follows:

Regimental Quick March of
The Loyal Regiment

THE RED RED ROSE

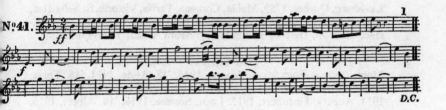

APPENDIX C

Battle Honours of The Loyal Regiment

Louisburg, Quebec, 1759, Maida, Corunna, Tarifa, Vittoria, St Sebastian, Nive, Peninsula, Ava, Alma, Inkerman, Sevastopol, Ali Masjid, Afghanistan, 1878–79, Defence of Kimberley, South Africa, 1899–1902.

THE GREAT WAR
Mons, Retreat from Mons, Marne, 1914, '18, Aisne, 1914, '18, Ypres, 1914, '17, '18, Langemark, 1914, Gheluvelt, Nonne Bosschen, Givenchy, 1914, Aubers, Festubert, 1915, Loos, Somme, 1916, '18, Albert, 1916, Bazentin, Pozières, Guillemont, Ginchy, Flers Courcelette, Morval, Ancre Heights, Ancre, 1916, Arras, 1917, '18, Scarpe, 1917, Arleux, Messines, 1917, Pilckem, Menin Road, Polygon Wood, Poelcappelle, Passchendaele, Cambrai, 1917, '18, St Quentin, Bapaume, 1918, Lys, Estaires, Bailleul, Kemmel, Béthune, Scherpenberg, Soissonnais-Ourcq, Drocourt-Queant, Hindenburg Line, Epéhy, Canal du Nord, St Quentin Canal, Courtrai, Selle, Sambre, France and Flanders, 1914–'18, Doiran, 1917, Macedonia, 1917, Suvla, Sari Bair, Gallipoli, 1915, Egypt, 1916, Gaza, Nebi Samwil, Jerusalem, Jaffa, Tel 'Asur, Palestine, 1917–'18, Tigris, 1916, Kut-al-Amara, 1917, Baghdad, Mesopotamia, 1916–'18, Kilimanjaro, E. Africa, 1914–'16.

SECOND WORLD WAR
Dunkirk, 1940, North-West Europe, 1940, Banana Ridge, Djebel Kesskiss, Medjez Plain, Gueriat-El-Atach Ridge, Djebel Bou Aoukaz, 1943, Gabgab Gap, North Africa, 1943, Anzio, Rome, Fiesole, Gothic Line, Monte Gamberaldi, Monte Ceco, Monte Grande, Italy, 1944–45, Johore, Batu Pahat, Singapore Island, Malaya, 1941–42.

Note: Those Battle Honours in bold type are emblazoned on the Queen's and Regimental Colours.